About this Learning Guide

Shmoop Will Make You a Better Lover*
*of Literature, History, Poetry, Life...

Our lively learning guides are written by experts and educators who want to show your brain a good time. Shmoop writers come primarily from Ph.D. programs at top universities, including Stanford, Harvard, and UC Berkeley.

Want more Shmoop? We cover literature, poetry, bestsellers, music, US history, civics, biographies (and the list keeps growing). Drop by our website to see the latest.

www.shmoop.com

Table of Contents

Introduction

In a Nutshell

Brideshead Revisited was published in 1944 by already famous British novelist <u>Evelyn Waugh</u> and based loosely on his own experiences as a student at <u>Oxford University</u>. The novel tells the story of a young man at Oxford captivated by an eccentric young man and his very wealthy, Catholic family. Like the narrator and protagonist of *Brideshead*, Waugh ignored his studies, lazed away his days in the company of aesthetes and drunkards, and focused on his personal writing and art at the expense of his grades and reputation. Waugh was an unlikely member of the <u>Royal Marines</u> and on a leave of absence when he decided to write *Brideshead*. He finished the first 60,000 or so words in fewer than three weeks, and completed the novel in about four months.

Reading *Brideshead* is about equivalent to sitting down for a five course meal. The narrative abounds with lush descriptions of food of every kind and lots and lots of expensive booze. (Waugh was on limited rations while writing the novel, so you might chock these results up to wishful thinking.) On top of that is the vivid portrait painted of architecture, interior design, and art of all kinds. It's certainly a trip for the senses.

This literary gluttony certainly caught the attention of the critics, as did the novel's rendering of the British aristocracy and Catholicism. At the time Waugh was writing, the golden age of aristocracy was coming to a close, and the novel has received criticism for glorifying classism. As far as religion goes, Waugh tried to present Catholicism positively and reflect his own reasons for converting to it; yet many interpret the novel in the *opposite* light, believing that religion actually brings about the ruin of every character in the story. How does it strike you?

Why Should I Care?

We don't know if you're closer to high school or college graduation (or done with school completely), but we're guessing that you're at least familiar with the concept that school has an endpoint. And what's weird about graduation is that it's always kind of sad that you've ended an era of your life, whether you're glad to leave or not. That's why we here at Shmoop all trooped off to see *High School Musical 3*. Sure, <u>Zac Ephron</u>, and <u>Vanessa Hudgens</u> may be good looking, and the dancing is to die for, but what we really wanted was the *nostalgia* we feel for that lost past.

In a way, *Brideshead Revisited* is like an ode to that moment in senior year when everyone knows that the end of a certain way of life is coming. For some (like, maybe, the Marchmains of the novel), the best years of their lives are already past, the years when they were, say, the captains of the football team or the homecoming queens (if English aristocrats can be compared to high school football captains). What's left after the end of this golden era, for some people, could be a slow decline: alcoholism, adultery, and even death.

We know that *Brideshead Revisited* isn't *literally* about high school. Still, if *Friday Night Lights* is anything to go by, a lot of people look back on their high school years as a period of glory before the anxieties of adult life. And it's pretty clear that Charles Ryder is doing something similar, looking back on those years before World War II as an "enchanted garden," the last gasp of aristocratic gentility and art for art's sake before the chaos of his post-Oxford working life.

What's going on in *Brideshead Revisited* is the graduation of an entire society, represented in miniature by one family, the Marchmains. We see this family transition from a state of relatively stable social grace to a period of instability and decay. But, just as there really is life after high school, there's some hope at the end of *Brideshead*. Even as the estate of the novel has fallen apart, among its fragments there are still some remains of earlier, better days that continue in tougher times.

Summary

Book Summary

The novel's narration begins in the first person with Captain Charles Ryder of the British Army (which he disdains) in the early 1940s. His troops have just arrived at their new camp, a large and beautiful estate called Brideshead Castle. Over the course of a flashback, Charles recounts his long and complicated history with the estate and the Flyte family that owns it.

It all starts at the beginning of Charles's first year at Oxford University in 1922. Charles himself is from a wealthy family that includes his caustic father and older cousin Jasper, who advises him on what to study, where to eat, and whom to avoid in his early days at the University. Charles soon makes the acquaintance of Sebastian Flyte, an extremely wealthy, quirky, beautiful young man who obeys his every impulse, shirks his duties, charms the pants off everyone, carries around a teddy bear named Aloysius, parties like a rock star, and makes his first introduction to Charles by leaning his head into our narrator's first-floor dorm room window and puking up several bottles of wine. The two boys quickly become the best of friends, much to Jasper's exasperation (since Sebastian hangs out with "the wrong crowd" – partiers and not scholars).

Among Sebastian's unorthodox friends is Anthony Blanche, a flamboyantly gay international playboy. Anthony takes Charles aside and tells him all about Sebastian and his family. Sebastian's parents, Lord and Lady Marchmain, are separated. Lord Marchmain lives in Italy with his mistress Cara. Lady Marchmain, a very devout Catholic, refuses to get a divorce and lives at the family's large and ornate country estate, Brideshead, as well as their home in London, called Marchmain House. Sebastian has three siblings: a stuffy and religious older brother, the Earl of Brideshead (simply called "Brideshead" or "Bridey"); a sister Julia who is a clever and self-indulgent beauty; and a younger sister Cordelia.

It soon becomes clear that Sebastian has major family issues. First of all, he struggles with the Catholicism his mother has so intently forced on her family. He also remains in close contact

with his father, which Lady Marchmain seems to read as betrayal.

Charles and Sebastian spend the first summer away from Oxford together, at Brideshead. Charles briefly meets Sebastian's sister Julia, but is largely alone with Sebastian for the duration of the vacation, getting quietly drunk every evening on the estate's astounding wine collection. Because Charles is a burgeoning artist, he is in constant awe of the architecture and interior design of Brideshead Castle. He devotes quite a bit of text to describing it in detail, and interprets his summer there as a time he was "very close to heaven." During his stay he also meets Cordelia, Sebastian's energetic and playfully troublemaking little sister, as well as Sebastian's old Nanny, who for some reason still lives on the estate. When Sebastian's brother Brideshead comes to dinner, Charles confirms that he is very much as Anthony Blanche predicted: stuffy, restrained, and grave. Religion seems an inevitable topic of conversation among the Flytes, especially when Charles, a self-proclaimed agnostic, is around.

Towards the end of the summer, Charles and Sebastian travel to Venice to visit Lord Marchmain (Sebastian's father) and his mistress Cara. Cara provides some useful information for Charles: Lord Marchmain despises his wife and everyone who loves her; that's why he's left England. Cara adds that, while Charles drinks controllably and to have a good time, Sebastian drinks to drown his sorrows and is fast becoming an alcoholic.

The second year at Oxford, Anthony Blanche is absent, having decided to stay and party in Munich instead of returning to school. Charles pursues his interest in painting, and Sebastian continues to drink. Meanwhile Lady Marchmain, nervous about her son's position at the university, comes to visit. She tries to befriend Charles to get him on her side in "helping" Sebastian. She also employs the help of Mr. Samgrass, a professor at Oxford, in trying to keep her son under control.

Soon after, Julia comes to visit, bringing with her a man named Rex Mottram who is suave, politically connected, and rumored to carry a gun. (He's Tony Soprano meets James Bond, but he's a bit of a wannabe.) Rex takes Sebastian, Charles, and one of their university friends, Boy Mulcaster, to a party. The Oxford guys sneak away to party at a club of ill repute and end up arrested for drunk driving. Rex gets them out of jail via his smooth-talking people skills. But because Sebastian's family is so revered as part of England's old aristocracy, his arrest makes for quite the scandal. Lady Marchmain cracks down, and both Sebastian and Charles end up stuck with a curfew back at Oxford, courtesy of Mr. Samgrass's authority. Needless to say, they both hate Samgrass.

Meanwhile Charles notices that Sebastian's drinking has indeed taken a turn for the worse. Though Lady Marchmain continues to try to keep Charles in her good graces, he ultimately chooses to side with Sebastian "against the world." Lady Marchmain gets fed up and pulls Sebastian out of Oxford, sending him off with Mr. Samgrass to tour around Europe.

Cut to Christmas at the end of the year. Charles is at Brideshead estate again with Sebastian and Samgrass, who have just returned from their European travels. Though it was Samgrass's job to keep Sebastian sober and out of trouble, Charles soon discovers that he actually lost Sebastian, or rather, that Sebastian gave him the slip in order to drink himself silly. Meanwhile, at Brideshead, Lady Marchmain has instructed all the servants to not give Sebastian any

alcohol. Charles feels bad for his friend and gives him money to buy booze. When Lady Marchmain finds out, she guilt trips Charles, who leaves when Sebastian tells him he's no use around here anyway.

When Charles returns to Oxford, Rex Mottram visits him and explains that he wants to marry Julia. Lady Marchmain is against it, since he is about 15 years older than her daughter, not of noble blood, and of suspect business dealings. Also, he's been sleeping with a married woman named Brenda Champion. Rex adds that Lady Marchmain has gotten very sick but refuses to see a doctor on account of her religion.

At this point the narrative time is disrupted and we get information in a scattered order through various flashbacks on Charles's part. The quick and dirty is as follows: Julia agrees to marry Rex, though he has to convert to Catholicism first. They find out just before the wedding that Rex was married and divorced once, which means he can't be married as a Catholic after all. They have a brief Protestant ceremony instead, to Lady Marchmain's horror.

In the meantime Charles bumps into Anthony Blanche, who updates him on Sebastian: still a drunkard and worse than ever. Sebastian has also struck up a close friendship with a German sergeant. When Charles hears that Lady Marchmain is dying, he hurries to see her at Brideshead, where she apologizes for being so harsh about his siding with Sebastian against her. Then, at her request, Charles sets out to find Sebastian and bring him back to Brideshead to say good-bye to his mother.

Charles travels to Morocco and finds Kurt, the German sergeant with whom Sebastian is living. It's clear that Kurt is taking advantage of Sebastian and using him for his money. Sebastian himself is ill in the hospital and, when confronted, defends his friendship with Kurt. He likes that, for once, he can finally take care of someone else, when all his life his family has been taking care of him. Then word arrives that Lady Marchmain has died.

Now we jump forward a few years. Charles is now a professional architectural painter – he paints people's houses, usually before the buildings are torn down for one reason or another. He's married, but we don't know who his wife is yet. After tiring of British architecture, Charles traveled to South America to paint there. Then he met up with his wife to take a ship back to America. She's just had their second baby, whom Charles hasn't met yet and has no interest in seeing. The honeymoon is clearly over between these two, and Charles is basically masking (poorly) some intense hostility for his wife. We finally discover that the wife is Celia Mulcaster, sister to Boy Mulcaster, one of Charles's friends from Oxford.

Meanwhile, Julia Flyte is also on this ship back to England and, during a violent storm at sea, she and Charles begin a passionate affair. This is problematic, since Julia is also married (to Rex) and also hates her spouse. It soon becomes clear, however, that both Celia and Rex have been adulterous in the past. So both Charles and Julia decide to get divorced and marry each other.

While staying at Brideshead estate together, Julia's brother Bridey visits and announces that he's getting married himself, to a widow who is apparently not attractive and has kids from her first marriage. Cordelia has returned home as well, bringing with her news of Sebastian. Kurt got

himself arrested by the Germans and hanged himself; Sebastian drank in distress and ended up begging a monastery in <u>Tunis</u> to take him in. She predicts that her brother will live out his days there, trying to be holy and repeatedly lapsing into alcoholic binges until his liver gives up and he dies.

Both divorces (Charles's and Julia's) are in progress when Lord Marchmain announces that he's dying and wants to live out his last days at Brideshead. He arrives with his mistress Cara to do so. When alone with Julia and Charles, he admits that he met Bridey's new wife, Beryl, and despises her. He doesn't want her living at Brideshead, so, although it's tradition to leave the estate to the eldest son, he wants Julia and Charles to have it instead. Charles is a bit ashamed by his own joy at this prospect.

However, it never comes to fruition: Julia decides that in order to be a good Catholic, she needs to make a sacrifice, and she chooses to sacrifice her happiness with Charles. They break up shortly after her father's death, which involves a heated debate over whether or not they should force the old man to see a priest. (Lord Marchmain was adamantly against religion). Charles, despite his previous agnosticism, is moved by the way Julia's father receives the priest at his deathbed. Somehow or another Charles ends up a Catholic himself by the time we pull out of the flashback and return to him as a Captain in the Army revisiting Brideshead. The novel ends with Charles examining the estate and reflecting with optimism on the flame still burning in Brideshead's little chapel.

Prologue

- It's <u>World War II</u> and your narrator, Captain Charles Ryder of the British army, along with the rest of the troops, is leaving his camp of three months and moving to a new location. It's just becoming spring.
- Charles remarks that he has no pleasant memories of the place – that here "love [has] died between [him] and the army."
- Ryder's troops are somewhere in the United Kingdom and, though Charles speaks of trams coming in from Glasgow, we can't be sure of exactly where they are. The camp stands at the outset of a city, around a farmhouse which would have been destroyed had the army not come to it.
- Not too far from the camp is a lunatic asylum, which gets its fair share of jokes from the passing soldiers. Charles mentions his newest platoon commander, named Hooper, thinks the madmen should be gassed.
- Charles explains that when they marched in during the Winter, the men were hopeful; rumor had it they were finally going to the Middle East. But, as time passed, it became clear that, once again, they weren't going anywhere.
- Charles couldn't help them, he says, couldn't cheer them up when couldn't even help himself. He's thirty-nine, and beginning to feel old. He goes to bed early, drinks a lot, and never wants to go out and party.
- He reiterates that his last love died here – his love for the army. He simply woke one morning and realized that their relationship was like a stale marriage. He had no more affection or interest holding him to the army, only duty and regret at having bound himself to her "in a moment of folly."

- That's why, on this spring morning, as the troops ready to move away from this camp of three months, Charles doesn't really give a hoot where they're going. Not that they're told anyway, since the army is all about tactical secrecy.
- Ryder imagines what an archeologist might some day say upon finding their remains, stripped of all adornments, like badges, again for purposes of secrecy: this was a primitive society with no identifying markers, etc.
- The sergeant-major points out to Captain Ryder a broken window which, like all other destruction in the camp, is attributed to the wind in the night.
- Hooper, the new platoon commander, shows up. Charles explains that most of the troops don't like Hooper, but that he himself holds a feeling of near-affection for the man, having to do with a very cute anecdote and a forced haircut.
- Hooper "holds no illusions about the army." He has simply *accepted* it. He has no romantic notions, which Charles imagines has to do with a very unromantic childhood, devoid of all bedtime stories and heroes' myths. He's just a logical, 'only the facts' kind of guy. He sleeps soundly, Charles concludes, while Charles himself lies awake "fretting."
- In Ryder's mind, Hooper is the symbol of Young England. He uses Hooper to test any generalized statements about "youth" he hears in the news or cocktail chatter.
- Anyway, as Hooper comes shuffling up, Ryder chastises him for being late and sends him to inspect the lines. After he's gone, Charles's superior, the commanding officer, arrives and gives Charles a hard time for the broken window and for a store of buried bric-a-brac, belonging to a soldier, which he finds in the ground.
- Ryder marches along with Hooper and the men discuss how they don't know where they're going, but that it's probably not "the real thing." (Meaning no fighting, just more traveling and camping and getting yelled at for broken windows.)
- On the train, Charles sits in a private carriage with three other officers. Partway through the day they are summoned to the C.O.'s train, reprimanded for their attire, and chided for the state in which their camp was left. Charles pauses to wonder if the man really uttered such phrases as are repeated here, or if in his recollection he has made them up.
- What follows is a lovely, satirical rendering of the way the army does things. The C.O. talks of moving "between location A and location B" with a series of halting, titled announcements. The gist is that Charles's troops – also known as Company C – will be unloading and setting up a new camp at their new (undisclosed) destination.
- During the night, Charles writes a useless and fictional report about the train being sprayed with mustard gas, in order to make the commanding officer happy.
- By four in the morning the men have reached their new location, at the outset of a large estate with a big house and a few lakes, set up a perimeter, and readied the camp.
- The next morning, after he wakes, Charles asks his second-in-command what the name of this place is. When he hears, he's shocked. Charles walks outside and observes the scenery, a man-made landscape with which he is intimately familiar. A stream named the Bride leads to a farm a few miles away called Bridesprings, where Charles used to have tea. (Curious…) The nearby Avon river has been dammed to form three lakes, surrounded by woods and other picturesque nature stuff.
- The house is there, Charles knows, but hidden by the woods. He wonders what is real, in this environment, and what is a mirage.
- Hooper comes along and tells Charles of a Roman Catholic church on the estate where a very small (as in, two people) service is taking place. Charles knows about the church, and the great fountain next to it. As he tells Hooper, he has been here before, and he knows all

about it.

Book One: Et in Arcadia Ego, Chapter One

- The first time Charles went to Brideshead was twenty years before, in June, with Sebastian. Flashback, here we come.
- It's Eights Week – a major rowing event – at Oxford, so the campus is packed with crew-loving guests. Among them are women, a.k.a. bait for the college men.
- Charles wants none of it. Rather than entertain the ladies, he's going out.
- Before he does, he discusses the impending evening ball with his servant, Lunt.
- By the way, this is 1923. Charles was good enough to mention as much a few paragraphs into this grand recollection.
- Anyway, Lord Sebastian soon arrives, dressed elegantly and remarking on the uproarious state of Charles's college, which is simply "pullulating with women." He's brought a car borrowed from a friend named Hardcastle, a bottle of wine, and a basket of strawberries. He and Charles soon take off with the intent of visiting Sebastian's "Hawkins." (You find out who this is soon.)
- In the car we meet Sebastian's teddy bear. (No, we're not joking. Yes, he's a grown man with a teddy bear. Just roll with it.) Aloysius sits between them; Sebastian instructs Charles to make sure the bear doesn't get sick as they drive.
- As they drive along pleasantly, Sebastian touches on Hardcastle, the owner of the car, who it seems is quite a partier/late-sleeper. He also mentions his own father, whom he calls "a social leper."
- At about eleven Sebastian pulls over to a picturesque side-of-the-road spot, and the young men lie around eating the strawberries, smoking, and drinking the wine. (Life is so hard.)
- Sebastian says that he would like to bury a crock of gold – here and everywhere else he's ever been happy – so he can return to it someday when he's "old and miserable," dig it up, and remember how things used to be.
- This day, explains Charles, was during his third term at Oxford, but he doesn't think of his Oxford life as having started until the day he first met Sebastian.
- It all stemmed from Charles having a first-floor room. At the very beginning of his time at Oxford, Sebastian's older cousin, Jasper, comes to give him a little chat.
- Having been at Oxford himself for some time, Jasper feels qualified in lecturing from an older, wiser, and annoying standpoint.
- Since Charles's father tends to avoid any serious chats with his son, Ryder has until now been spared this sort of agony. The most Mr. Ryder said to his son is that he was allowing him 550 pounds a year as an allowance, only because the Warden recommended no more than 300 and twice as much as that would have been "deliberately impolite."
- But back to Jasper. In his lecture, he covers every possible Oxford base: how to dress, what lectures to attend, which clubs to join now and which to join next year, how to make his reputation, which places to avoid, which *people* to avoid (*especially* religious folk), and adds that Charles will likely spend his second year getting rid of the "undesirable" friends he will make in his first.
- Jasper also advises that Charles change his rooms immediately, rooms which are beautiful

and Charles happens to love. First floor rooms are a bad idea, he says, since people will start dropping in left and right – especially those *undesirable* people.

- Charles says that he never followed any of this advice, at least not consciously. He kept his first-floor rooms and decorated them with Van Gogh prints and the like. He formed a circle of friends, among them a man named Collins, who "maintained a middle course of culture between the flamboyant 'aesthetes' and the proletarian scholars who scrambled fiercely for facts." Yet, despite excellent rooms and a solid circle of friends, Charles felt Oxford had more to offer.
- Then there was Sebastian, who made everyone else fade into the background. Collins was once explaining to Charles the problem with modern aesthetics, but his eyes were not open to art until Sebastian declared that he feels the same emotion for a butterfly that he does for a cathedral.
- Sebastian was one of those guys that everyone knew. Not as a personal friend, that is, but they knew who he was. He was just that beautiful, Charles says, and just that eccentric. The first time Charles saw him, he was carrying…his large teddy bear. Charles was getting a haircut at the time and so received a description from the barber, who reported that Sebastian was the son of The Marquis of Marchmain and had an older brother, the Earl of Brideshead, who has finished his time at Oxford. Also, the teddy bear's name is Aloysius.
- Ryder was at first rather judgmental, thinking Sebastian an odd duck. Not that we can blame him.
- Anyway, the night they met, it was under less than ideal circumstances. It was early March, around midnight. Charles was entertaining some guests and had opened his first-floor windows for air. Sebastian, extraordinarily drunk, was wandering by with some of his own friends. He staggered over to Charles's room, leaned in the window, and threw-up *into* Ryder's room. His friends apologized on his behalf before carting him off to bed.
- The next morning, Charles comes back from class to find his room full of flowers "in every conceivable vessel in every part of the room." His servant Lunt informs him that Sebastian left a note, as well, in which he apologizes and declares that his bear isn't even speaking to him. He also invites Charles to join him for lunch, without leaving an address, since everyone knows who he is and where he lives.
- That luncheon turned out to be a new beginning for Charles, though the details are now confused in his mind with other almost identical get-togethers that would follow. He arrived at the lunch "in search of love" and "full of curiosity," looking for the entrance to what he imagines as some sort of secret garden at Oxford.
- Sebastian was alone in his room when Charles arrived, eating plover's eggs and looking beautiful. His room was full of a fascinating hodge-podge of objects.
- The lunching party begins to assemble, which includes a few freshmen and one Anthony Blanche, a ridiculous character who, as scholars say, embodies every gay stereotype of Waugh's era. He also speaks with an affected stutter. Charles calls him the ultimate aesthete, "ageless as a lizard, foreign as a Martian." Charles enjoys Anthony immensely.
- After they lunch together, Anthony goes out on Sebastian's balcony and recites passages from T.S. Eliot's *The Wasteland*, sobbing them out across the campus below. Anthony is equally enthusiastic about Sebastian having "discovered" Charles.
- As the lunch party breaks up, Charles and Sebastian are once again left alone. Sebastian declares that he *must* go to the Botanical Gardens, and Charles accompanies him to see the ivy.
- When he gets back to his rooms, they suddenly seem superficial to Charles. He dislikes

most the painted screen, which he turns to face the wall.

- And now we return to Charles and Sebastian, during Eights Week at Oxford, lying under the tree, eating strawberries, and drinking wine.
- After the snack by the side of the road, the boys drive on and find themselves at Brideshead, which Sebastian describes not as his home but as the place where his family lives. They're away at the moment, but Sebastian wants Charles to meet his Nanny – Nanny Hawkins.
- They meet; she's an older, serene woman who informs them that Julia, Sebastian's sister, is at Brideshead for the day and should be returning from lunch shortly. As she and Sebastian go on chatting, Charles takes his time observing the domed room and its décor.
- Sebastian is in a hurry to get himself and Charles away before Julia returns. His family is so charming, he explains, that they'll meet Charles and take him away, make him their friend instead of Sebastian's.
- Charles submits, but is eager to see more of the spectacular house and grounds. Sebastian takes him to see the chapel, "a monument of art nouveau." When they enter, Sebastian crosses himself and genuflects (kneels on one knee), which Charles does in suit. But Sebastian is cross, and says he need not copy him just for good manners.
- He shows Charles around, explaining that the chapel was a wedding present from his father to his mother.
- On the way out of Brideshead in their car, the young men pass a chauffeured Rolls-Royce which Sebastian declares is Julia returning home. They got out just in time, he says.
- During the drive back, Sebastian apologizes for being snippy – Brideshead has that effect on him.
- (Charles explains, in his narration, that Sebastian always works in imperatives. Everything he does he *has* to do, like going to see Nanny or visiting the botanical gardens.)
- The men discuss families: Sebastian doesn't like his; Charles doesn't have much of one (just him and his father, as his mother was killed during World War I).
- Looking back on that day now, Charles is amazed that so small of an event – his first visit to Brideshead – is recounted now "with tears by a middle-aged captain of infantry."

Book One: Et in Arcadia Ego, Chapter Two

- At the end of the summer term, Charles gets another visit from Jasper – the last visit from Jasper, he adds.
- Jasper gives yet another lecture, but this one full of disappointment rather than hope. He tells Charles that he's fallen in with the very worst group of undesirables in all of Oxford. Sebastian Flyte may be OK, but Anthony Blanche is certainly not.
- Jasper also slips in some info about Sebastian's family. His parents, the Marchmains, have lived apart since the war ended. They're still married because Sebastian's mother is a Roman Catholic and refuses to get a divorce, but her husband now lives in Rome while she stays in England.
- He moves on to discuss Charles's allowance, which he's certain Charles has exceeded, based on the lavish paraphernalia lying around his room. Among other things is a human skull from the school of medicine with the words *Et in Arcadia ego* inscribed on its

forehead. (Make sure you read about this in "Symbols, Imagery, Allegory.")

- Jasper continues, reprimanding Charles for his clothes and lack of extracurricular activities. Ryder hasn't made a name for himself, and this gravely concerns his older cousin. Also, Jasper says, he's been drinking too much.
- That's Charles's cue to interrupt his cousin, insist that he likes his lot of bad friends, spending double his allowance, and, most of all, drinking. He then invites him to join him for a drink, though it's only the afternoon.
- Jasper would later write to his father about the matter, who would write to Charles's father, who would do nothing about it.
- And then it was time for the Easter vacation, which Charles spent with Collins in Ravenna. Ryder wrote letters to Sebastian and received two back, written "in a style of remote fantasy." Collins falls into the world of art that would later lead to his career. Charles wonders, in reflection, whether he might have gone the same way as Collins had it not been for Sebastian.
- Instead, Sebastian has given him the happy childhood he never had when he was actually a child. Looking back, despite Jasper's lectures, there is nothing he would have done differently. If he had cared enough to engage with his cousin, he would have told Jasper that "to know and love one other human being is the root of all wisdom."
- And now we shift the spotlight to Anthony Blanche, with whom Charles has been spending a lot of time. Anthony is, as Ryder says, "a nomad of no nationality." He had a peculiar upbringing in a variety of locations all over the world, where he met and became close with the most famous of writers, philosophers, and thinkers. He's done and seen everything.
- Anthony may be experienced, but he pursues vice and wishes to shock those around him. He's still savage and cruel, and in that way is still very young.
- And then he asks Charles to dinner, alone, where he is loud and attention-seeking. Before they go they stop for Alexander cocktails (frothy drinks with cream) which Charles finds to be disgusting.
- Anthony tells a story from a few nights prior, in which he was in his pajamas and reading until disturbed by a mob of twenty or so rowdy boys outside in the piazza chanting his name. They knew him as a friend of Boy Mulcaster, who Anthony says is known as the perfect example of "a degenerate."
- It seems Mulcaster spent Easter with Blanche and his family and made a spectacle of himself – surprising, since he is a Lord and this is not a great display of English aristocracy. He lost all his money at cards and Anthony had to pay for everything.
- Anyway, Anthony leaned out the window and made some mocking remark to Mulcaster, who was with this rowdy crowd. A bunch of them came clattering up the stairs, and one boy accused Anthony "of unnatural vices." Anthony very wryly remarked that he couldn't handle all these boys at once and that the impertinent one had better come back alone.
- The boys then tried to "put Anthony in Mercury," which refers to the pond with a statue of Mercury on campus. (In other words, they were going to chuck him into the water.)
- Then Anthony remarked that nothing would give him more please than to be "manhandled" by these "meaty boys."
- And that does it. No one really wanted to throw him in the fountain after that. So Anthony got in on his own, after inviting them to watch him bathe.
- He remarks to Charles that something like that would never happen to Sebastian; he is too charming. The next day he went to see how Sebastian was and found him with two of the rowdy crowd from the night before, who were there to see how the teddy bear was.

Sebastian had only sympathy for the young men, even after he heard the story from Anthony.

- Back in the day, says Anthony, when they were younger, Sebastian wasn't so well-liked. He never used to get in trouble with the masters so the other boys didn't like that. He was also beautiful, and never had any "spots" (British for "pimples").
- He also used to spend a long time in the confessional, which baffled Anthony, since Sebastian never did anything wrong.
- He basically talks all through dinner, even inviting Charles to come to France with him and drink fabulous wine. He calls Charles an artist, having seen several drawings of his hidden away in his room.
- Sebastian doesn't understand Charles's artistic abilities, he continues, but those who are charming don't need brains anyway. Anthony feels as though he himself has squandered everything, and will never become, say, an artist, as Charles will.
- But back to Sebastian. The only question, says Anthony, is how such a lovely boy came from such a "sinister family."
- He proceeds to describe all of Sebastian's family. Brideshead, Sebastian's old brother, is deemed "archaic" and a "learned bigot." Julia is smart and incredibly beautiful, but "a fiend—a passionless, acquisitive, intriguing, ruthless killer" who is interested only in power. There's another sister, but she's still young. The mother, he says, is very elegant, while her husband is large and powerful, handsome and slothful. Society has rejected him, and none of his family but Sebastian will go to see him.
- He talks some more about Lady and Lord Marchmain's awkward estrangement, now that he lives in Rome. Fifteen years into their marriage he went to war and came back with a mistress. His wife refused to divorce. Anthony knows all this, he explains, because he was in Venice when both Lady Marchmain and Lord Marchmain were around.
- Anthony is clearly on Lord Marchmain's side, since the man has given his wife everything she could ever want, and let her keep both of their houses (Brideshead and Marchmain house) and all the staff so she can "suck their blood," as Blanche so delicately puts it. Even Adrian Porson – a companion of Lady Marchmain's – used to be "the greatest, the only poet of [the] time" until she got to him.
- That's why you can't blame Sebastian for any shortcomings, he says, like being insipid (lacking zest). He never remembers anything the boy says for more than five minutes, and finds that Sebastian's comments remind him of a painting called "Bubbles."
- He compares Sebastian to Stefanie, a duchess with whom Anthony claims to have had an affair. She was enticing until she became a habit and "boredom grew like a cancer." He recommends that Charles be wary of Sebastian, as being "strangled with charm" is not a good experience for an artist "at the tenderest stage of his growth."
- On the way home from dinner, Anthony says he's sure that tomorrow Charles will repeat everything he's said to Sebastian, and Sebastian will 1) not change his feelings for Anthony at all, and 2) immediately start talking about his bear.
- Charles returns to his room for a restless night, which he cannot blame solely on the drinking. He keeps hearing Anthony's words repeated.
- The next morning, Sunday, Charles eats breakfast and walks through campus amongst a horde of church-goers.
- When he arrives at Sebastian's place, the young man is out, so he sits and waits. Sebastian returns from church, where he sat up front so that Monsignor Bell, who's been writing home to tell Lady Marchmain that Sebastian hasn't been attending services, would

notice him.

- Charles asks Sebastian if Anthony has ever met any of his family. No, says Sebastian, as far as he knows, though he then admits that he remembers hearing something about Anthony being in Venice when his mother was there.
- Then Charles wants to know to know about the duchess, Stefanie, and if Anthony ever had a big affair with her.
- Certainly not, says Sebastian, though he thinks they were stuck in an elevator together once.
- Charles is convinced that Anthony was lying and tells Sebastian that Blanche spent all last night trying to turn him (Charles) against Sebastian. Sebastian finds this to be silly – as does his bear.

Book One: Et in Arcadia Ego, Chapter Three

- At the end of the year, Charles is out of money and won't receive more until October. This is a problem.
- Sebastian doesn't have much of an allowance himself, but gets everything he wants by asking his mother, who prefers that everything he has to be a present. Even talking about his mother makes Sebastian "retreat," as Charles says, into his own solitary world.
- Much of youth, says Charles, is made up of reflection and regret, though in adulthood we imagine our youth was dreamy and free of such melancholy.
- It is with such self-reproach that Charles spends his first day at home with his father – he felt regret at having overspent his allowance. His father spends the whole day in the library, and emerges only at dinner.
- Mr. Ryder is about fifty, but appears at least seventy. He wears an archaic smoking suit for dinner and always dines formally at home. He greets Charles, asks about the train home, and the two of them sit down to dinner.
- Charles remarks that he thought about taking a class at an art school during the summer vacation, but that he doesn't really have any money. His father remarks that he's the worst person to come to for advice, as he's never had that problem himself. He seems positively gleeful, and spends the rest of dinner reading his book while ignoring Charles.
- After dinner, Charles takes a second shot at it. He ventures that surely his father doesn't want him spending his entire vacation here at home? His father responds that, if he felt that way, he would never reveal as much.
- For the next week, Mr. Ryder spent all day in the library, and Charles spent all day brooding. Dinner was their "battlefield." Mr. Ryder insists that his son entertain him, Charles makes poorly veiled attempts at getting more money, and Mr. Ryder pretends to not understand the innuendo – though it's clear from their lavish, many-course dinners that money is no issue whatsoever for him.
- Then Charles provides us with some back-story. After his mother died, his aunt Phillipa – his father's sister – came to live with them for a while. She was a companion to Charles, but Mr. Ryder seems to have regarded her with menace. "I got her out in the end," he says of her now (she left the country by the time Charles went to Oxford), which Charles reads as a challenge to himself.

- Charles runs into a man named Jorkins, a friend from his boyhood days whom he never liked and whom he finds relatively unchanged now.
- Jorkins comes to dinner and serves as entertainment for Mr. Ryder, who decides to a play a little game pretending that Jorkins is American, but never makes references explicit enough that Jorkins can correct the misunderstanding.
- A few days later, Mr. Ryder throws a dinner party to check the monotony of a nightly meal with his son alone. Their guests are specifically designed, says Charles, to annoy him, and include Sir Cuthbert and Lady Orme-Herrick, Miss Gloria Orme-Herrick, her bald fiancée, and a boring publisher. It's awful.
- Charles's stay at home continues in this combative fashion, for his father loved this sort of battle, until he receives a letter from Sebastian, who has gone to Venice to visit his father. The letter's style reminds Charles of what Anthony said of Sebastian that night at dinner – that he was insipid but couldn't be blamed for it. For days after the letter, Charles thought he hated his friend Sebastian.
- Then he gets another letter in which Sebastian curtly declares he is dying. Charles leaves at once to visit him, informing his father of the situation on his way out the door. Mr. Ryder doesn't understand why Charles is in such a hurry, since he's no doctor and wouldn't be able to save his friend anyway. "Do not hurry back on my account," he adds.
- Charles is panic-stricken during his train ride to Sebastian, imagining what horrible accident might have befallen his friend. He is afraid that he will be too late, Sebastian already dead by the time he arrives.
- When Charles gets to Brideshead, he is met by Lady Julia – Sebastian's sister – who takes him by car to the house and informs him that Sebastian isn't dying, he broke a tiny bone in his foot by tripping over a croquet hoop.
- Now that he can relax, Charles notes how much like Sebastian Julia is. She resembles him, sounds like him, and speaks with the same manner of speech. He feels as though he knows her already, because he already knows Sebastian. The only difference is her being a woman, a trait he recognizes intensely.
- Julia has him light a cigarette for her, and there's a moment of sexual tension, at least for Charles.
- When they arrive at the house, they find Sebastian, in his pajamas, seated in a wheelchair with one foot all bandaged up. Charles simply says, "I thought you were dying" and realizes that, while he is relieved, he's also angry at Sebastian for having put him through that.
- They all have dinner in "the Painted Parlour," an ornate octagon room with wreathed medallions on the wall. Charles explains the war he's been fighting with his father.
- After dinner, Julia leaves to go see Nanny Hawkins. Sebastian declares that he loves his sister, that she's so much like him. Then he clarifies – she looks and talks like he does; he doesn't think he could love anyone with a character like his own.
- That night the two friends drink and walk around the estate, and Charles feels "a sense of liberation and peace."

Book One: Et in Arcadia Ego, Chapter Four

- Charles reflects on Youth, and more particularly, the languor or relaxation which goes with it. Languor belongs only to youth, he says, and can never be recaptured later in life. This is what he experienced that summer with Sebastian at Brideshead, and he believes he was very close to heaven in those days.
- Sebastian is discussing Brideshead Castle with Charles and explains that it doesn't really belong to him, since it is "full of ravening beasts" at the moment.
- Living at Brideshead is to Charles an aesthetic education, though Sebastian is unconcerned with the history or facts of the architecture and design. ("What does it matter when it was built if it's pretty?" he asks.)
- Sebastian convinces his friend to draw the grandiose fountain in the center of the terrace. He does, and at Sebastian's order gives it not to Lady Marchmain, but to Nanny Hawkins.
- Charles feels his aesthetic predilections shifting to the baroque as the summer continues.
- One day the young men find a set of oil paints and decide to decorate the office. Charles paints a romantic landscape, without figures, which comes out rather well, if he does say so himself.
- Some time later they realize there's enough old wine in the cellar to keep them quite happy ("enough" = 4 bottles a night between them) for the rest of the summer.
- Of course, the topic of religion soon arises. Charles himself has no religion, and always considered it a myth that had finally been exposed. But Sebastian was of course raised a strict Catholic, which he admits is difficult.
- Sebastian says he prays every day to be made good, but not yet. To Charles's great surprise, he believes in the story of Christmas and Jesus. He believes in it because it is "a lovely idea."
- Charles wants to know: if Sebastian believes in it all, where is the difficulty? But Sebastian only responds that if Charles can't see it, he can't see it.
- A week or so later, the young men are sunbathing on the roof when Sebastian reveals that his older brother, Brideshead, is coming home, and they shall have to hide to avoid him. He informs Charles that Brideshead is the craziest of all of them, and used to want to be a priest, and now he doesn't know what he wants. He was upset with their father's departure because the church doesn't believe in divorce.
- He then reveals that his father isn't much of a religious man anyway, and only converted to Catholicism in order to marry their mother. Charles should meet Sebastian's father, Sebastian says, as he's "a very nice man."
- Sebastian claims he's always been his father's favorite, and that he's the only one of the four children who doesn't hate him now.
- Religion has hit his family members in such different ways. But all Sebastian wants is happiness, and religion doesn't seem to have much to do with happiness.
- Catholics, he says, have an outlook on life completely different than that of other people. It's difficult to belong to this "clique," as he calls it, since he and Julia are both semi-heathens.
- Just then Cordelia, Sebastian's 11-year-old sister, comes clamoring onto the roof. Charles and Sebastian cover themselves up quickly (they were sunbathing, remember?).
- Like most 11-year-old girls, Cordelia does all the talking, mostly about her pig, named Francis Xavier, and the lovely new painting in the office (which Charles created), and how

they must come to dinner with her and "Bridey."

- Dinner gives Charles the opportunity to observe Sebastian's brother closely for the first time. Though Brideshead is only a few years Charles's senior, he seems much older, full of "gravity" and "restraint."

- Charles also hears that Cordelia is a troublemaker at her Catholic school, and reveals himself an agnostic, not an atheist.

- They begin discussing the church on the estate and whether or not it will be closed, since no one really uses it anyway. Brideshead asks Charles, as an artist, what he thinks of the building aesthetically. It's probably good art, he says, though he's loath to define that very term. He adds that, personally, he doesn't like it very much, which raises the question, from Brideshead, whether there's a difference between liking something and thinking it good.

- Charles reflects that this conversation reveals a division between himself and Brideshead; they will never really understand each other.

- After dinner, Brideshead whisks Sebastian away to deal with estate-related business, leaving Charles with Cordelia who, despite chiding from her brother, calls him by his first name instead of "Mr. Ryder." She tells Charles that, since he's an agnostic, she'll pray for him.

- She adds that, if he weren't an agnostic, he could buy a black goddaughter "from some nuns in Africa." You pay five shillings and they name a baby after you. She has "six black Cordelias already," a scenario she finds to be quite "lovely."

- Shortly after, Sebastian's siblings depart and leave him alone with Charles once again. They decide to go to Venice together and visit Lord Marchmain.

- Upon arrival, they are greeted by Lord Marchmain's valet, a man named Plender, who takes them by gondola to Marchmain's "palace."

- The place is bare, with little extraneous furniture, mosquito nets on the bed, and the bathroom built in where a chimney used to be.

- When they finally meet Sebastian's father, he seems rather normal – the tall, dark, and handsome type. Charles is also shocked at Sebastian's ease with his father (especially given Charles's own strained relationship with dad back home) and at Lord Marchmain's casual mention of a mistress, as though it were nothing.

- The mistress's name is Cara, and she's away visiting friends. The three men have dinner together, and Charles wonders that this man, who seems so young, is somehow the same age as his own father.

- The next day Charles meets Cara. He must have expected Julia Roberts in knee-high boots, because he's shocked to find a well-dressed, middle-aged woman, seemingly unmarked by social stigma.

- Cara acts as their tour guide around Venice, showing them all the tourist-y spots.

- The young men stay in Venice for two weeks, which passes dreamily. Charles is perfectly happy there. One night Sebastian looks up at a statue and declares that he and Charles can never possibly get involved in a war, which he finds to be sad.

- One day Charles finds himself alone with Cara, which gives her the opportunity to tell him about his friendship with Sebastian. It's a special relationship, she says, that exists between young men of their age – romantic friendships, a kind of love whose meaning isn't known to them yet. It's better, she explains, for young men to have that kind of love for another man before he has it for a woman.

- That was Lord Marchmain's problem, Cara says. His first love was Lady Marchmain, and

now he hates her. He doesn't even love Cara, but only stays with her to protect himself from his wife. He hates her so much, Cara says, that he can't even be in the same country as her. He can't bear to be around people who may have spoken to her recently or are headed in her direction. That's why he isn't social – not because he's been rejected by society, but because he refuses to be around those who run in the same circles as his wife.

- All this hate, she explains, comes from his having loved her before he was grown-up enough to do so.
- Meanwhile, she says, Sebastian is in love with his own childhood. He also drinks too much, which will ruin him. He has a certain way of drinking, different than Charles...
- The summer vacation ends, and Charles returns home to his father, who inquires about the weather. Later that night he asks about Charles's dying friend, about whom he was so worried.

Book One: Et in Arcadia Ego, Chapter Five

- When their second year begins at Oxford, things have changed. Sebastian feels old, he says, and he's been getting a series of talking tos from Monsignor Bell and Mr. Samgrass, who is his tutor and friend of his mother's.
- Charles feels middle-aged, as though they can't expect to have any more fun at Oxford.
- Anthony Blanche, meanwhile, has left. He's in Munich with some policeman to whom he's "formed an attachment.".
- Indeed, this second year is far less eventful than the first. Sebastian and Charles retreat into the shadows, so to speak. It's so boring that Charles even starts to miss his cousin Jasper – there's no one left to shock. After his gluttonous summer, he decides to settle down.
- In addition to his other studies, Charles joins an art school and produces what he deems worthless drawings in their twice weekly meetings. He starts dressing more appropriately and becomes a respectable member of his college.
- Sebastian is different; he retreats into solitude, grows more sullen and lacks energy. The pair spends more time together and gradually stops seeing the group of friends they made in their first year. He chalks some of this up to Anthony's absence.
- Not far into the first year, Lady Marchmain comes to visit. She tries to make Charles her friend, which is problematic for his relationship with Sebastian.
- Sebastian's mother is creating a memorial book for her brother, Ned, who has died in World War I and left behind a trove of historic documents. Mr. Samgrass is a history don (don = professor) and author himself, so he is helping her out with the endeavor. This is, supposedly, her reason for visiting the University.
- Charles indulges in some further description of Mr. Samgrass. He's one of those guys who spends his life sifting through archived documents. He knows everything about old British families of royal blood, the politics of the Catholic church and its members in the Vatican, old scandals, etc. Charles finds Mr. Samgrass to be in great contrast to Lady Marchmain.
- A few weeks later, Charles is alone in Sebastian's room, waiting for him to return, when Julia walks in with a man named Rex Mottram. The three of them and Sebastian all end up

having lunch together.

- Rex has a Canadian accent and is a forward, engaging man. He's done well with money, is a member of Parliament, and has curried favor with Important People. He never went to the University, because he didn't want to waste his life with education. In short, he's a businessman, to an extent. And he's thirty-ish.
- Julia treats him with "mild disdain" and "possession," but that's how she treats everyone.
- A week later Rex invites Charles, Sebastian, and Boy Mulcaster to a party of sorts. They head to Marchmain house (the Flytes' second home, in London, whereas Brideshead is in the country) to have some drinks beforehand, and it turns out that the party is a charity ball for one of Julia's organizations.
- When Julia arrives dressed for the ball, Charles describes her as "unhurried, exquisite, unrepentant." Take note, reader.
- The result of all this drinking beforehand and all this waiting for the women to dress and get ready is that everyone is quite drunk before they ever get to the function. Mulcaster tipsily suggests they sneak away and go to Ma Mayfield's, a totally sketchy joint in town where he "has" a girl named Effie.
- So shortly after they arrive at the ball, the three men – Charles, Sebastian, and Boy – sneak away. They walk the short distance back to Marchmain house to take Hardcastle's car (in which they drove from Oxford).
- Once they're in Ma Mayfield's, the men continue to drink (surprise!). Boy finds this girl Effie, who seems to not remember him, though she's more than happy to have him buy her food and drinks. Charles and Sebastian end up with two girls of their own, one that Charles refers to as Death Head and the other Sickly Child. The men end up leaving Ma Mayfield's, with all three women.
- Sebastian takes the wheel. This is a very bad idea. The women sense as much and leave the car, shortly before the men are pulled over and, after some drunken protesting on the part of Mulcaster, arrested.
- In jail, the men decide to call Rex, since he seems like the sort of guy who could handle a situation like this one.
- And handle he does. Rex shows up with enough Cuban cigars and hand-shaking charm to make the policemen happy. Clearly "rejoicing in his efficiency," he takes the three guys home to his place.
- The next morning they discuss the issue. Sebastian is in the most trouble, as he was driving drunk. They agree to submit to the charges and explain that they're simply good Oxford boys, unused to drinking wine (HA!).
- As they wait at the courthouse, Sebastian wants to go abroad. He'd sooner go to prison, he says, than deal with the downfall from his family (mostly his mother and brother).
- He and Charles meet up with Julia, who wishes they had taken her with them, as she's always wanted to see the Old Hundredth (the name of Ma Mayfield's club).
- She explains that Lady Marchmain isn't really upset, and wants to have lunch with Charles and Sebastian.
- So they do. Lady Marchmain seems to find the whole thing humorous, though she does worry over having to explain it to the rest of her family. Afterwards, Charles is relieved, not understanding why Sebastian still looks completely miserable.
- Because of the prestige attached to Sebastian's family name, the newspapers are all over the event. They publish the story with a headline: "Marquis's Son Unused to Wine" or "Model Student's Career at Stake" and a good chuckle is had by all who know better,

which by now includes us, the readers. Still, Sebastian gets off easy thanks to Mr. Samgrass's testimony that he is a fine individual.

- Back at Oxford, Samgrass uses more of his influence, unfortunately to "gate" Sebastian and Charles. (They are confined to their respective colleges as punishment. For definitions and other fun slang, check out Shmoop's "Links" page.)
- But the worst penalty, says Charles, was being forced into close acquaintance with both Mr. Samgrass and Rex Mottram.
- Samgrass, especially, has that annoying habit of turning every encounter into an intimate bond between himself and the boys. He starts visiting one or both of them every night, to check up and tell long, boring stories about his time at Brideshead and the people he meets, including Celia, Boy Mulcaster's sister, who is apparently "saucy." (More on her later.)
- During Charles's time at Brideshead over the Christmas vacation, Sebastian's mother continues to try to make him her friend. She talks of converting him to Catholicism, which doesn't help her in the friendship endeavor.
- Charles remembers bits of their conversations, including Lady Marchmain's personal history. She married into money and used to worry that being rich was wrong when so many people in the world were suffering, but then she realized that God favors the poor, so she was really suffering herself by being wealthy. (Life is so hard.)
- But despite these long, intimate talks, Charles remains firmly on Sebastian's side. He worries for his friend, who these days wishes only to be left alone. Charles compares him to a Polynesian native, happy and peaceful on his island until a big ship drops anchor at the shore and he is forced into battle with the rest of the world. Sebastian's time "in Arcadia" is limited, says Charles.
- He also begins to understand Sebastian's wary suspicions regarding his family and religion. When he can't stand his family anymore, Sebastian asks to go to London. Charles takes him back to his house, and Charles's father finds him "very amusing."
- Back at Oxford, Charles sees this sadness growing in Sebastian, but doesn't know how to help. Drinking gets to be an issue too – Charles recognizes that he himself drinks for the "love of the moment," but that Sebastian drinks "to escape." (Hmm, it's almost as if we've heard something like this before…)
- At Easter, they all head to Brideshead for the holiday. Sebastian is in a great depression and Charles cannot help him. Sebastian just drinks in the library, secretly, all day. He gets worse when the guests are gone and he has to face his family alone.
- One night he's too drunk to even come down to dinner and simply locks himself in his room. Charles covers for him, pretending he's just got a cold.
- When Charles tells Julia the truth, she doesn't seem to recognize the severity of the situation – she simply declares her brother "boring."
- Sebastian is sitting in Charles's room, plastered and openly resenting Charles "spying" on him for his mother.
- Down at dinner, Cordelia spills the beans to Lady Marchmain. The Earl of Brideshead deals with it in his own way – by being removed and declaring that you can't stop people when they want to get drunk.
- Some considerable time after dinner Sebastian comes down, even *more* plastered than before, to "apologize." NOT to his mother, he announces, but to Charles, his "only friend." Charles takes him back up to his room, where Sebastian starts weeping. He feels betrayed.

- The next morning Sebastian wants to leave Brideshead – along with Charles. But Ryder isn't comfortable with just running away and not saying good-bye, so he lets Sebastian leave without him and promises to meet his friend in London. This leaves Charles alone at Brideshead – with Sebastian's family.
- Charles finds Lady Marchmain, who is distraught not by Sebastian's drunkenness the night before, but by his depression. She doesn't know why he left without saying good-bye; Charles explains that her son is "ashamed of being unhappy."
- This has all happened before, says Lady Marchmain – with Sebastian's father. He used to drink the same way, and he used to run away the same way. He, too, was ashamed of being unhappy.
- Then she asks for Charles to help Sebastian – because she can't. She also asks Charles to take a look at her brother Ned's memorial book – the one she's been putting together with Mr. Samgrass.
- Charles realizes that Lady Marchmain is manipulating him, trying to get him to betray his friend. Later that morning, as he leaves Brideshead, Cordelia comes out and asks him to give Sebastian her "*special* love."
- In the train on the way to London, Charles looks over the book that Lady Marchmain gave him, and we get some background on her family. She doesn't look anything like her three brothers, and is older than the oldest brother by nine years. She also has two sisters.
- The book itself is a series of letters, journal entries, and photographs, all revolving around her now dead brothers. He wonders if Lady Marchmain is going to die soon as well.
- When Charles reaches London, he finds Sebastian as youthful and as cheery as when he first met him. Sebastian knows Charles has talked with his mother, and he asks if Charles has gone over to her side.
- No, says Charles, he is with Sebastian, against everyone else.
- When they return to Oxford, Sebastian's depression kicks in again. They find a flat to share for the upcoming term. When Charles bumps into Mr. Samgrass, however, the don tells him not to commit.
- Sebastian admits that his mother wants him to live with Monsignor Bell. As soon as Lady Marchmain knew she'd failed getting Charles on her side, she started a new plot.
- Then she comes to visit, and stops for lunch with Charles. She wants to know if Sebastian's drinking too much. Charles says no.
- So of course that night Sebastian gets hammered and is found by a junior dean stumbling around campus at 1am. Apparently he's gotten into a habit of drinking alone *after* Charles departs for the evening.
- Charles is angry with Sebastian for having made him look like a liar to Lady Marchmain. He also thinks it's ridiculous for Sebastian to drink every time his family is around.
- Charles tries to explain to Lady Marchmain what happened, but she insists it's no use, that there's nothing to be done about a drunkard's lies.
- She also worries that Charles is Sebastian's only friend – that there are no Catholics for him to hang about with. He's not strong enough to keep his faith alone, she says.
- She explains that Sebastian's college will allow him to continue only if he goes to live with Monsignor Bell; Charles counters that this will make Sebastian drink himself silly. He'll be miserable, and he's someone who needs to feel free.
- That night Sebastian confirms this, alone with Charles. He's going to visit his father in Italy instead of putting up with this garbage at Oxford. And then they get roaringly drunk together. Again.

- The next day Sebastian leaves with his mother. Charles is left to converse with Brideshead (who also came to Oxford for this ambush). Charles insists that, were it not for religion, Sebastian would have had a chance to be happy.
- That night Charles goes to visit Collins, one of their buddies from the first year, to fill the void Sebastian left. He can't.
- At the end of the term he returns home and asks his father if he wants him to finish his degree. Of course not, says his father, it's no use to either of them.
- So Charles decides he wants to be a painter.
- Shortly thereafter, Charles receives a letter from Lady Marchmain, explaining that Sebastian has gone to stay with his father and will be chaperoned around Europe by Mr. Samgrass after that. He may come back to Oxford after next Christmas.

Book One: Et in Arcadia Ego, Chapter Six

- We open with Charles, Julia, Cordelia, Lady Marchmain, Brideshead, and Sebastian back at Brideshead castle, two days after Christmas.
- Mr. Samgrass is narrating the events of his travels with Sebastian.
- It's clear that something is up. Sebastian isn't in the pictures, and Samgrass insists that it's because he was holding the camera. Charles can tell there's something that he's not willing to tell Lady Marchmain.
- Oddly enough, Anthony Blanche is in one of the photos; they bumped into him in Constantinople and he traveled with them to Beirut.
- Sebastian himself looks weary, thinner, pale. Charles is concerned for his health.
- Ryder tells his friend all about his time in art school in Paris. He is not impressed with the students or the teachers, and agrees with Cordelia that modern art is "bosh."
- As they wait for dinner, Sebastian rings for Wilcox to bring drinks – but he's busy having an intimate conversation with Lady Marchmain.
- Brideshead finally corners Charles alone to tell him that his mother doesn't want Sebastian drinking. Apparently Mr. Samgrass lost him over Christmas and found him again the night before.
- This is apparently all in vain, as Charles finds Sebastian alone in his room, drinking.
- Shortly after Charles finds himself alone with Julia, who's still treating Sebastian's alcoholism with casual annoyance. She mentions that there's something fishy about Mr. Samgrass but that her mother only sees what she wants to, and adds that she herself is causing trouble for the family, too.
- That night at dinner, Sebastian asks for whiskey and is given half a glass. It's one of those tension-filled family dinners with which we're familiar.
- Brideshead talks about hunting the next day, and Sebastian adds he'd like to go as well, much to everyone's surprise. (Wait for it...)
- Later, Sebastian explains to Charles that he plans on ditching the hunting as soon as they all split up and spending the day at a pub in town. (There it is.)
- Then he asks for money, the better to drink at a pub with. He has none of his own and even pawned his watch for cash when he was abroad. He tells all about his time with Mr. Samgrass and the various ways he managed to escape the man's company.

- The next morning, Charles concedes and gives Sebastian two pounds before he heads off to the hunt.
- Ryder is left alone at the house with Samgrass, who attempts to keep up the charade regarding a supposedly successful Christmas break with Sebastian.
- But Charles is having none of it; he knows the truth, he says, and it's clear that he's not willing to discuss his friend with this jerk.
- Samgrass explains that Sebastian can't possibly get into any trouble today because he has no money and no one would possibly be wicked enough to give him some. (Oops.)
- Then Julia enters and explains that Rex is arriving today. She asks if Charles is going to paint another medallion on the wall of the garden room, since he has done one on each of his visits to Brideshead (there are now three completed).
- Julia brings up Sebastian; if he's going to get drunk all the time, she says, he should go away somewhere else. It's clear to Charles that she's more concerned with embarrassment for the family than she is about her brother's severe depression.
- Then Lady Marchmain puts in her two cents. They have to keep Sebastian with them, or accompanied by Mr. Samgrass. Charles knows but doesn't say that Sebastian will run away again – just like Lord Marchmain did – because he hates her just like his father does.
- Then Charles talks to Brideshead, who manages to bring what Charles considers to be religious overtones into the mix. If he ever felt like becoming a Catholic, Charles says, talking with Bridey would have been enough to convince him otherwise.
- And now for some comic relief. Rex has arrived with a Christmas present for Julia: a small tortoise with Julia's initials set into the living shell in diamonds. Lady Marchmain appropriately wonders if it eats the same thing as normal tortoises. Mr. Samgrass wants to know if they'll fit another tortoise into the shell when this one dies.
- Rex also has a solution for Sebastian: ship him off to a guy he knows who fixes this sort of problem, in Zurich.
- Cordelia comes back from the hunting party, ravenous and reporting that Sebastian is "in disgrace."
- Sebastian calls the house, asking to be picked up from a hotel bar. When he gets back "two-thirds drunk," Lady Marchmain lets him drink more.
- After a drunken dinner Sebastian goes to bed, drunk, as you might have guessed.
- The next morning, Charles asks if his friend if he wants him to stay at Brideshead. No, says Sebastian – Charles is no help.
- So Ryder goes to say good-bye to the family. When Lady Marchmain gets him alone, he admits to having given Sebastian money the day before.
- She calls Charles "cruel" and "wicked," but sounds more disappointed than angry.
- Charles is unmoved by Lady Marchmain. He drives away from Marchmain house and feels as though he's left some part of himself behind him. He commits to never go back and declares that he's left behind a world of illusion to move into a real world of real dimensions, to be experienced with the five senses.
- In retrospect, Charles says that there is no such world – but he did not know this at the time.
- So Charles returns to Paris, thinking he's done with Brideshead.
- Not so much. He gets a letter from Cordelia three weeks later. She is sorry he went away and isn't angry with him for slipping Sebastian money because, quite honestly, she's been supplying him booze herself. She also reports that Samgrass is gone and that Julia and Rex are getting very close, much to her dismay. Also, Rex is taking Sebastian to that

fix-all German doctor.

- Oh, and the diamond-encrusted tortoise buried itself to die.
- About a week later, Charles gets back to his rooms to find Rex waiting for him. It seems that, on the way to Zurich, he has lost Sebastian.
- Rex has come to see if Sebastian is with Charles, but Ryder declares he is done with that family. (Oh, just wait.)
- The men go out to dinner; it's Charles's job to order and Rex's job to pay. Eager to make Rex happy, Charles orders an elaborate, many, many course dinner.
- Charles asks about the news from Brideshead: did everyone talk about him after he left?
- Yes, said Rex. A few days after his departure, Julia realized Samgrass was a fake and called him out on having lost Sebastian and failing at his chaperoning duties. That was the end of Samgrass at Brideshead, and Lady Marchmain regretted having given Charles such a hard time.
- Then when, they realized Cordelia had been slipping Sebastian whisky every night, they figured it was time to do something drastic. Meanwhile Lady Marchmain is very sick and refuses to get treatment – maybe something to do with her religion, suspects Rex.
- Rex explains that they are in trouble financially, too. They're overdrawn 100,000 pounds in London (you don't even want to think about how much money that was in the 1920s).
- As Rex goes on about the state of Sebastian's family, the dialogue is interspersed with Charles's monomaniacal (obsessive about a singular thing) comments about the meal. If you're reading, you'll be full by the end of the chapter.
- Speaking of money, Rex would like to marry Julia, sooner rather than later. Lady Marchmain doesn't want this to happen, because Rex isn't from the same class as Julia, and because he's not a Catholic.
- Also, he's been carrying on an affair with a prominent society woman named Brenda Champion, from whom he's derived all his social and political connections. So there's that.
- Anyway, since Lady Marchmain won't bite, Rex is headed to Italy to get Julia's father to approve the marriage.
- Dinner has progressed to the cognac. Rex doesn't like it and has them bring out something better, which he also vetoes. Finally they bring out the good stuff, to Rex's satisfaction. Charles busies himself with his own drink and ignores the rest of Rex's words.
- In May, Rex and Julia's engagement is announced; in June they are married quickly and quietly without a big affair – which is not the way Rex wanted things to go.

Book One: Et in Arcadia Ego, Chapter Seven

- Charles begins by speaking of Julia. In the early years of when they knew each other, she was only slightly intrigued by him, but she caught his interest because of her likeness to Sebastian.
- He recalls the first time he met her, in 1923, when Sebastian had his supposedly fatal foot injury and she picked Charles up at the railroad station. She was eighteen and at the center of the London aristocratic social scene.

- Charles knows that the night Julia met him, she had no interest in him. She was in her own little world, wondering whom to marry, and, as Charles was not a contender, he had no place in her thoughts.
- Not that she really cared about whoever she was going to marry – an arranged partnership would have been just fine with her.
- While Julia was the best catch of her friends, she still lost points for a few issues: her father's scandal, her religion. For a variety of reasons, many different categories of men were unavailable to her. Tragically, she had to hunt out those who are suitable.
- So Julia created in her mind the perfect man for her: thirty-two, recently widowed, a great political career ahead of him, "mildly agnostic" but OK with a Catholic household, etc. So when Julia met Charles by the train station, she knew he was not her man.
- Charles learned all this gradually, he explains, over the years that he knew her. He learned it the way one learns the life of a woman he loves…
- Julia thought more on this imaginary perfect man, whom she called "Eustace." The problem is, he became a sort of joke to her, so that when she did meet a man just like the imaginary "Eustace," and he fell in love with her, she sent him away.
- Oh.
- Julia liked the fact that Rex was much older than she. Dating older was the chic thing to do among her friends. He knew the right people, he had money, and there was a mysterious air of danger about him, as though he were involved in something illegal. (Tony Soprano syndrome.)
- She also liked that he was carrying on an affair with socialite Brenda Champion. That made him far more appealing to her. (Charles interprets it this way: Julia sensed that Brenda was the kind of woman she might become, and she fostered a rivalry between Brenda and herself for the affections of Rex Mottram.)
- Charles delves back into his narrative at the time when Rex and Julia haven't yet started dating. They're in France; Julia is staying with her aunt, Lady Rosscommon, and Rex is staying nearby…with Brenda.
- Rex is getting tired of Mrs. Champion. He wants a more exciting life, and Julia seems as good a prize as any to go chasing after. Of course, there's not much he can do in the way of courtship, considering he's living with another woman at the time, but he "establish[es] a friendliness."
- Lady Marchmain hears about said friendliness and warns Julia to stay away from Rex, since he's not very nice. Julia responds that no, he's not, but that she doesn't entirely like nice people.
- Once they are both in London together, Rex shamelessly pursues Julia. He plans his entire life around her – always trying to show up where he thinks she might be, ingratiating himself with her family, driving her anywhere she wanted to go, etc. He becomes indispensable to her, and then she falls in love with him.
- Then, one evening, Rex tells Julia he's busy and can't see her. She finds out later that he was with Brenda. The next morning, she refuses to see him, ignores all his phone calls, and stands him up for lunch.
- Finally, Rex comes by the house. Julia says she doesn't want to see him, but her mother insists that she be polite and not just "take people up and drop them" this way.
- So Julia talks with Rex, alone, and agrees to marry him. Her mother is not pleased, but Julia explains that the only way she could justify her jealousy and anger was if she and Rex were officially involved.

- Lady Marchmain starts plotting to fix the situation. She tells Julia not to speak of the engagement to anyone.
- Meanwhile, Julia and Rex "made love." Note: Some think that this term means sex, and others maintain that, during this time period, it didn't necessarily mean rounding home base. Take it as you will. Either way, Julia finds "making love" with Rex more enjoyable than previous encounters with "sentimental and uncertain boys." But then she remembers that she's a Catholic, and this sort of pre-marital passion is not OK. She puts an end to the monkey business.
- So Rex gets it somewhere else, namely from Brenda Champion. Julia tries explaining this to her priest – that she should be allowed to commit a small sin (pre-marital sex) to prevent Rex from committing a larger one (adultery).
- The priest is having none of it.
- So Julia is having none of the priest, or her religion for that matter. She drops Catholicism like a hot potato and gets back into bed with Rex.
- Lady Marchmain, who now has an alcoholic son, a sexually active daughter, a husband living with another woman in Italy, and an inappropriate future son-in-law, continues to go to church on a daily basis.
- As the year continues, it gets harder and harder to keep the engagement a secret. In her despair, Lady Marchmain plans to forbid the marriage, close Marchmain House, and take Julia away for six months.
- That's when Rex goes to Italy to visit Lord Marchmain who, upon hearing that his wife detested Rex, immediately consented to the marriage.
- There's some trouble with the lawyers when Rex wants to have Julia's dowry to manipulate for himself – he doesn't want it tied up in trustee stock because he's used to using money to make money (that's sort of what he does).
- Then there's the religion problem. Rex is Protestant, but cheerily agrees to convert to Catholicism as though he were changing his socks. Lady Marchmain dismally remembers her own husband converting, with equal nonchalance, when she was married.
- Rex doesn't want to learn anything, he just wants to sign the form that says he's Catholic. Lady Marchmain explains that it doesn't quite work that way and sets him up to meet with a priest.
- Rex plays along. 'Whatever you say, father" is his general mantra, but it's obvious he's just trying to please. The priest declares him impossible (he sees right through the cheerful veneer), but finally submits and makes Rex a Catholic.
- In the meantime, Cordelia has been telling him all sorts of fairy-tale lies about Catholicism, like everyone having to sleep with their feet pointing east so they can walk towards heaven if they die. She calls Rex a "chump" for buying her crock.
- Then, three weeks before the wedding, Brideshead announces that the wedding is off. It seems that Rex was already married and divorced.
- Rex thinks it's no big deal; he married young and divorced long ago – why should it matter? Julia explains that Catholics don't believe in divorce. OK, says Rex, he'll get an annulment; just tell him how much it costs.
- What must be several painful days of banter later, Rex understands that he can't make this problem go away. So he decides to get married in a Protestant church.
- Lady Marchmain tries to argue, but Julia just declares that she's been sleeping with Rex for some time, and if they don't get married she'll just keep on being his mistress.
- And that's the end of Lady Marchmain for the night; she hobbles up to bed.

- Years later, Charles asks Julia why she would tell her mother that. Julia explains that she was so deeply involved with Rex she couldn't just call the whole thing off. She wanted to make "an honest woman" of herself. Plus, she was only twenty.
- Rex got permission from Lord Marchmain to have a Protestant wedding and that was that.
- It was a "gruesome" wedding, she says, and no family from her mother's side attended.
- Cordelia was disappointed that she didn't get to be a bridesmaid after all. She found Julia, begged her not to get married, and then said she hoped Julia would be "always happy."
- Then Julia comments that the priest who tried to convert Rex to Catholicism understood him best: he "wasn't a complete human being." Julia didn't realize this until a year after they were married.
- This is what she said to Charles, ten years after her marriage, in a storm on a ship in the Atlantic.

Book One: Et in Arcadia Ego, Chapter Eight

- Charles comes back to London in May of 1926. His father is "delighted" to have him back "so soon," though he's been away fifteen months.
- That night he dines out with his new gang and bumps into Anthony Blanche and Boy Mulcaster. Anthony is taunting Boy, who's considering going to the Old Hundredth later – in short, nothing has changed.
- Anthony takes Charles aside and they discuss Sebastian (like we said, nothing has changed). Anthony explains that Sebastian came to live with him in France after parting ways with Charles. He drank all day long and even stole and pawned two of Anthony's suits for cash for more booze.
- Anthony tried to help him with his alcoholism problem, it would seem, by getting him into other activities/substances instead. "If you want to be intoxicated," he says, "there are so many much more delicious things [than alcohol]." (It's unclear whether the man Anthony sends Sebastian to is a male prostitute or a drug dealer.)
- But Sebastian writes a bad check to the supplier of these activities and/or substances, which is bad news, in the mobster's-coming-after-you sort of way.
- Mulcaster rejoins them and Anthony continues: he went to Tangiers with Sebastian and met his new friend, the German, who shot his foot to get out of the army. Anthony wasn't a fan, so he left them and came back to England alone.
- Mulcaster, not entertained by the conversation, leaves to ring the fire alarm, so as to liven things up.
- Anthony reveals that Sebastian and his friend went to French Morocco – he thinks they were in trouble with the police in Tangiers. Since he's come back to London, Sebastian's mother has been badgering him to try and get in touch with her son.
- Because Mulcaster has prank called an alarm, two fire engines pull up just as he and Charles leave the nightclub. Mulcaster remarks that he doesn't think a lot of Anthony, and the two of them spend the night talking about the war.
- The conversation results in Charles's decision to join a flying squad in London. He sees action only once, when a group of young rebels attacks a few policemen. That's about it. Then the General Strike is called off, and there's not much to do after that.

- Julia hears that Charles is in England again and contacts him; Lady Marchmain is ill and wants to see him, she says.
- Charles hurries to Marchmain House in London, where he meets Julia and is informed that Lady Marchmain is dying.
- Julia tells him that her mother is terribly sorry for being so "beastly" to him with regards to Sebastian's drinking. She also wants to know if Charles can help fetch Sebastian to the house now.
- Before he goes to bed for the night, Charles learns that Brideshead didn't help England with the General Strike problem and that Cordelia is there in London as well, helping to take care of her mother.
- So Charles takes off in search of Sebastian. He travels to Fez (in Morocco) and dines with the British Consul to find out about his friend.
- The Consul is pleased that someone has finally come to take Sebastian off their hands. He likes the boy, it's just that Sebastian needs something to do with himself. He's also still hanging around with the German guy, who is a big leech.
- Charles heads to Sebastian's place and notes the Moroccan scenery as he travels. Back then, says narrator Charles, he thought it was suburban and modern. But thinking back on it now, he finally understands what holds Sebastian here.
- When Charles enters what he is told is Sebastian's residence, he finds the German that he's heard all about, listening to jazz music and sitting in a chair with a bandaged foot. One of his front teeth is missing and he speaks with an amusing lisp.
- The German informs him that Sebastian is ill and in the infirmary. He then explains a brief history of his own life, which involves joining the army and then shooting himself in the foot to get out. He adds that his foot is full of pus. Thanks.
- Charles explains that Sebastian's mother is ill; the German hopes that this will mean more money for them to spend.
- So Charles heads for the hospital, which is being run by Franciscan brothers. He discovers that Sebastian is recovering from the grippe – he is OK but not exactly fit for traveling.
- The Franciscan with whom Charles converses has been completely taken in by Sebastian, whom he praises for never complaining and for taking in the poor German soldier with a foot full of pus.
- Finally, Charles is taken to see his friend. He notes that Sebastian looks "emaciated" and run down. Sebastian explains to him that, these days, he just couldn't manage if he didn't have Kurt.
- Charles breaks the news about Lady Marchmain, but Sebastian simply calls her a *femme fatale*.
- Charles continues to visit Sebastian as he heals; Sebastian continues to get his friend to sneak him in alcohol. This concerns the doctor, who blames Sebastian's sickness on the alcoholism to begin with.
- Then the men receive word that Lady Marchmain is dead. Sebastian still hesitates to return to England, because he's not sure if Kurt would like it there. He explains that he's been taken care of his whole life, and he likes that now he finally has someone to take care of himself.
- So Charles takes Sebastian back home, where he immediately begins waiting on Kurt though still so ill himself. Charles also arranges the finances so that Sebastian's funds are limited to a weekly allowance and so that Kurt won't drain him of his money. Then he goes to London to finish these financial affairs.

- In London Charles meets up with Brideshead, explains the situation, and gets him to agree to this new plan for Sebastian's money.
- Then Brideshead explains that Marchmain House is being pulled down, and his father would like four oil paintings of the estate to commemorate it. Charles agrees to create the paintings, works as quickly and possible, and ends up producing what are still four of his favorite works.
- While he paints, Cordelia comes by to watch. She is older now (fifteen) but not as beautiful as Julia.
- Charles takes her out to dinner and they talk about Sebastian. He realizes that Cordelia knew more than he thought she did. She professes that she loves her brother "more than anyone."
- She informs Charles that the chapel at Brideshead was closed after her mother's requiem.
- She wishes Charles could understand the affinity people feel for their place of religious worship, and quotes this line: *Quomodo sedet sola civitas*.
- (Note: This is the first line of a religious chant. It means "How the city sits alone…" The next line is *pleno populo*, which means "which was full with people." Celia is describing the chapel which, once full, has now been closed.)
- This, of course, launches Cordelia into yet another religious conversation. It seems as though members of her family have left God, but this isn't so, she says. Cordelia quotes a priest and claims that, though Sebastian and Julia may wander from their religion, they are forever held by a string tying them to it. They can be brought back any moment "with a twitch upon the thread," she explains.
- She goes on to talk about her mother. She was closer to her than her siblings, but she doesn't think she ever really loved her. (Yikes.) She adds that "when people wanted to hate God, they hated [Lady Marchmain]."
- Cordelia hopes that she has a vocation, so that she can become a nun. Her brother Brideshead wishes he had one, but he doesn't.
- Charles, meanwhile, has no interest in this religious chatter. He "felt the brush take life in [his] hand that afternoon," he says. He is so inspired by the work he's done on the paintings that he can think of nothing but art.
- And the first half of the novel ends with Cordelia asking for another meringue.

Book Two: A Twitch Upon the Thread, Chapter One

- Charles begins with a long, ornate discussion of memory. Memories are mysterious, he says, unexplainable. He compares them to those times in history when civilizations that have always been peaceful and constructive suddenly fall apart through violence and crime.
- While we're on the topic of large-scale abstractions, he adds that every man keeps company with different versions of himself. We end up getting swept through life without our permission until we take the time to pause and reflect.
- This is what happened to Charles – his friendship with Sebastian is the time he felt the most alive.
- After that part of his life was over, Charles became an architectural painter. He paints

buildings because he thinks they are greater than the men who built them. He was often commissioned to paint great houses which, in part due to economic decline, were about to be destroyed. (The same way he painted Marchmain House).

- Charles travels to Central America to paint the architecture there. While he's gone, he makes little attempt to stay in touch with those back in England.
- His work abroad is a great success; the critics praise Charles, but his wife (!), while thinking the paintings brilliant, doesn't believe they are quite him.
- Charles meets up with his wife in America, noting that she left "her son" at home and remembering vaguely some mention of her new daughter.
- His wife is surprisingly unperturbed at the fact that Charles forgot he now had a second child. She explains that she named her daughter Caroline, because that is the female equivalent of "Charles."
- While the two of them lie in bed that night, Charles's wife asks him if he still loves her; he evades the question.
- In narration, Charles explains that he married his wife six years before, and that she helped launch his artistic career. They own a house in "her part of the country" in England.
- Charles's wife (we still don't know her name) explains that she had their barn turned into a studio for Charles to paint in. He is reticent and unappreciative.
- When she asks if Charles got her letter about boy, we are told (parenthetically, no less) that Boy Mulcaster is her brother. (Now is when you flip all the way back to the middle of Chapter Five and find that Boy Mulcaster has a sister named Celia.) Celia explains that Boy was going to marry some horrid girl but that Johnjohn, with all the wisdom of youth, somehow talked him out of it.
- Celia remarks that she and Charles can pick up where they left off two years ago when he went abroad. They forget about the incident which is now all over and forgotten. (Hmm.)
- We cut to Charles and Celia on their ship back to Europe. Celia is popular with the Americans, so their cabin is full of gifts (flowers, books, etc.) wrapped in cellophane.
- When she decides to throw a cocktail party that night, the first person she calls is a mutual friend who is also aboard – Julia Mottram.
- Charles hasn't seen Julia for several years, since the day he got married. In fact, he hasn't seen any of the Flytes since then. As far as he knows, Sebastian is still abroad and Julia and Rex are unhappy together.
- Charles explores the ship and concludes that wealth here is vulgar compared to what he saw in Central America.
- He bumps into Julia while walking around the ship. They have drinks together, and Julia remarks that she never sees Charles or anyone else that she likes anymore. He finds it odd that she acts as though they were great friends when they left off, when in fact they never knew each other very well.
- He asks what she's been up to, and Julia answers that she thought she was in love with someone, but "it didn't turn out that way." Charles feels she's grown up considerably, gained a humility that she never had before.
- Julia tells Charles that he's changed, grown "harder" than the youthful boy he used to be.
- In his narration, Charles remarks that Julia is nearly thirty and just about as beautiful as she will ever be, which has a lot to do with the sadness she now possesses. He also mentions "the love [he is] soon to have for her."
- Charles returns to his cabin and describes his and his wife's rooms: they've been given a large VIP suite due to his wife's ability to garner favor with important people. Also, the

chief purser has sent a life-size swan carved out of ice and filled with caviar that is now dripping into a silver dish.
- It's clear that Celia is blissfully unaware of what really happened in Book I. She callously refers to Sebastian as a "dipso" and is somehow under the impression that her brother dated Julia.
- Celia reminisces about the night she got engaged to Charles; he reminds her that she was the one who popped the question.
- Charles's wife explains that she's invited some Hollywood people to the party, so that he can break into the scenery-design business. Charles isn't exactly enthusiastic about the prospect.
- So Charles suffers through his wife's cocktail party, concerned only with when Julia will arrive.
- He begins conversing with an eccentric little redheaded Englishman vacuuming up the caviar. This scene is essentially like the wild party in *Breakfast at Tiffany's* , except that no one is drunk and they're all far less interesting.
- At last the party begins breaking up, while everyone talks about the impending storm they will surely suffer through.
- Shortly after, Charles and his wife go to dinner, where they are seated at the Captain's table. Julia is there as well and explains that she couldn't come to the party because her maid had disappeared and she had nothing to wear.
- Diner conversation is absurd and aristocratic and full of good old Waugh-style mocking humor. You should read it if you feel like a British laugh or two.
- Charles can't handle it, especially since he's just come back from the jungles of Central America. He believes that he is like King Lear on the heath.
- Then the impending storm finally arrives – Charles notes that Julia, like himself, is relieved to have the dinner broken up. Everyone clears out until Julia, Celia, and Charles are left alone at the table. Julia remarks that this is like King Lear, which is amazing and not at all contrived to show kindred between her and Charles. They banter that the three of them are like the three characters weathering the storm together in Lear – the Fool, Kent, and Lear himself.
- Celia doesn't get it.
- The three of them head to the lounge, which is nearly empty, and then go back to their cabins for bed. During the night, Celia is sick from the tossing of the boat, and Charles can think of nothing but Julia.
- The next morning, Celia is still sick and essentially confined to the cabin all day. He has one of their flower bouquets sent to Julia, and she telephones him for what seems to be the sole purpose of bantering over the phone and arranging to meet before lunch.
- When they meet, Charles and Julia walk around the promenade together. He bonds with her over the fact that they are both seemingly immune to the storm. She is the only woman they see out and about.
- Julia says she's glad Charles sent her the roses this morning. They were a shock and made her think they were "starting the day on quite the wrong footing." Charles knows what she means and expresses (in narration) that the love he and Julia will share is always based on this sort of communication.
- They end up lunching with a gentleman they meet while wandering the ship. This new guy likes Julia and thinks that she and Charles are married. Charles finds this amusing.
- They all return to their respective cabins to take a nap. That night, they meet again to

attend a party thrown by the gentlemen who thinks they're married. A group of them end up in Charles's sitting room to play roulette.

- Charles and Julia spend the entire next day together, too. At one point they make out in her room, though later that night she refuses to have sex with him. "I don't know if I want love," she says.
- Charles explains that he's not asking for love, but Julia insists that he is.
- Julia and Charles talk all night; this is where he hears the whole story of her past, including her marriage to Rex and all the technical problems that went with it (because of the conversion and his prior marriage). There was also some messy business around whether or not they should have a child, and their baby was ultimately born dead.
- Julia says that Rex isn't "intentionally unkind," it's just that "he isn't a real person at all." Two months after their honeymoon was over, he was sleeping with Brenda Champion again – worst of all, he couldn't imagine why it hurt Julia for him to do so.
- Charles partakes in the "share my pain" session; he says that he was happy when he found out Celia was having an affair, because it meant that he was justified in disliking her. (Ouch!)
- Julia wants to know why he married Celia (good question). Charles responds that she was the ideal wife for a painter, that he was lonely, that he missed Sebastian, etc. He calls Sebastian "the forerunner" and says that "Julia understood" what he meant.
- (Note: it sounds to us like he's referring to Sebastian as the forerunner to Julia, or rather, his relationship with Sebastian as the forerunner to his relationship with her.)
- Charles hears more news of Julia's family, too. Lord Marchmain remains in Venice, Sebastian has "disappeared," Cordelia is working as a nurse in Spain, and she and Rex live at Brideshead, with her brother.
- Rex is disappointed with Julia as a wife; he writes her off completely until someone he thinks is important takes a liking to her. Despite all this, she's been faithful to him…until now.
- Julia adds that, although she has lost religion herself, she wanted to raise her daughter as a Catholic when she thought she was going to have a baby. Of course, Rex didn't mind that the baby was stillborn since it was a girl. Julia feels she's been punished somehow for marrying Rex.
- The next day, after some accidental storm-induced physical contact while wandering the deck, Charles and Julia finally sleep together in her cabin. He stays the night, and the next day the storm is essentially over.
- That morning Charles makes his way back to the cabin and finds his wife awake and feeling much better. She makes a joke about him picking up other women. When he responds that he spent the time with Julia, Celia remarks that she "always wanted to bring the two of [them] together." Hardy-har-har.
- That night they all have dinner together at the Captain's table. Celia looks beautiful, and Julia no longer looks sad.
- Before they leave the ship, Charles and Julia make plans to meet again in London.
- As the voyage draws to a close, Celia wants Charles to come home with her so he can see their new daughter, Caroline. But Charles insists that he needs to go to London for his work.

Book Two: A Twitch Upon the Thread, Chapter Two

- It is the day of Charles's private exhibition of the paintings he did in Central America. Celia has arranged the whole thing in an attempt to please the critics as much as possible. During the preparation, Charles phones Julia and works out the details for what seems to be their impending romantic get-away.
- When he meets up with Celia, she says she's just been speaking with this guy Mr. Samgrass about Brideshead Castle. Charles remarks that the man is a crook.
- Celia is not pleased when Charles says that he's going to Brideshead that night. She wants him to stay at home with her, and adds that he hasn't seen his daughter Caroline yet.
- The exhibition begins and Celia sets to charming everyone, explaining to the critics that Charles lives for Beauty, was tired of finding it "ready-made" in England, so went off to Central America to create it for himself.
- After lunch, an important critic who had dismissed Charles in the past finds him and says of his new work, "I knew you had it. I saw it there. I've been waiting for it." Others applaud the work as "virile" and "passionate," words that have never been used before to describe Ryder's work.
- Charles recalls that this week of his exhibition was also the week he detected that his wife was cheating on him. He felt that this knowledge freed him, somehow, and that she could not hurt him anymore.
- At the end of the day, Celia remarks that she "wish[es] it hadn't got to happen quite this way," which Charles takes to mean she knows what's up.
- Just then Charles hears a loud, dramatic voice at the entrance protesting that one shouldn't need an invitation to come in and see the art. It is Anthony Blanche, and he hasn't changed at all.
- Anthony senses that all is not well in Charles's love life, so he whisks him off to a shady bar to hear of his "other conquests."
- As they sit together at the bar, Charles feels as though he is back at Oxford again. Anthony narrates his own reactions to Charles's work. He found the earlier English works to be very charming, but not his own cup of tea.
- Then he heard about Charles's new work, which was described to him as "barbaric" and "unhealthy." Naturally, this sparked Anthony's attention, and he rushed off to the exhibition at once. (Meanwhile, his conversation with the socialite Mrs. Stuyvesant Oglander revealed that Charles and Julia were having an affair, which means everyone knows about it.)
- When he arrived to see the paintings, continues Anthony, he found that they weren't as "barbaric" as everyone claimed. They seemed to him like "simple, creamy English charm, playing tigers."
- Charles agrees with this assessment.
- Anthony explains that this is why he took Charles out to dinner that night back at Oxford – to warn him of the dangers of charm, which he believes kills everything, including art and, by now, probably Charles as well.
- Charles leaves Anthony at the bar and meets Julia on a train headed for Brideshead, as planned. He tells her that his wife knows about their affair. Julia just says that it had to happen eventually, and that it doesn't matter if Rex knows or not because he isn't a real person and doesn't really exist.

- At Brideshead Charles finds Rex and several of his friends, annoying politicians with loud voices and over-inflated egos. Charles notes that these men all fear Julia.
- That evening, Charles listens to them all banter over current socio-political events. Later, he and Julia wonder whether it's worse listening to this political chit-chat or dealing with Celia's art and fashion.
- Charles wonders why it is that his love for Julia makes him so hateful (of everyone else). They decide that they are happy in their isolation together, but when Julia declares that they can't be hurt by others now, Charles forebodingly asks "for how many nights" that will remain the case.

Book Two: A Twitch Upon the Thread, Chapter Three

- Charles is painting a portrait of Julia (which he "never tire[s] of doing") one afternoon at Brideshead. They haven't seen each other in about a hundred days, as they've been keeping up appearances for the sake of Celia's children, as she requested.
- Charles and Julia recall all the times they've met in secret over the last two years, in various locales all over the world. It's clear that they're in love with each other.
- Julia says that she wants to marry Charles so that she can have "a day or two [...] of real peace" with him. She knows this will take some planning, not to mention a divorce or two. Julia says she "feel[s] the past and the future pressing so hard on either side that there's no room for the present at all." (Paging Jay Gatsby!)
- That night, the happy [adulterous] couple is surprised to hear from the butler that Julia's brother Brideshead has arrived from London. Charles notes that Brideshead is somewhat of a mystery, having managed to do nothing concrete with his adult life except become a famous collector of match-boxes.
- When he arrives, Charles notes that, although 38, he looks about 45 as he's grown heavy and bald. He declares that he has something to say, but wants to wait until the three of them are alone (without the servants).
- Brideshead, in what Charles calls his typically "preposterous yet seldom [...] absurd" manner, says that if he were a painter, he would paint action pictures, like battle scenes.
- Then he asks where his mother's jewels are, and Julia explains that they are in the bank.
- Finally, after dinner, when the three of them are alone, Brideshead announces that he's going to be married. Julia wants to know if she's pretty. Not exactly, he says. She's big. And her name is (attractively) Mrs. Beryl Muspratt. She's a poor widow with three children. Her dead husband collected matchboxes, which is how they met in the first place.
- Julia and Charles congratulate him, then ask why he hasn't brought her to Brideshead with him.
- Brideshead explains that it doesn't matter to him if Julia wants to "live in sin" with Charles, but that Beryl is a woman of "strict Catholic principle" and would never stay under the same roof as such activity.
- Julia leaves the room in tears. Charles tries to tell Brideshead off, but he is emotionless in return.
- Charles goes looking for Julia and finds her outside, sitting at the fountain. Julia explains that she's not upset at her brother; she's upset because what he said is true. Then she

rants about what it means to live with your sin constantly.

- While she speaks of religion, Charles feels distant from her.
- They go to her room and she freshens up her face after all that crying. They go back downstairs to join Brideshead, who acts as though nothing happened.
- He explains that he and Beryl are moving into Brideshead, which of course means that Rex and Julia have to move out.
- Later, Charles tries to tell Julia that religion is bunk; Julia wishes that it was. She discloses that Sebastian has gone back to the church himself. She feels as though she's too far gone, but thinks she should try and put her life in order, which means marrying Charles and having a baby with him.
- They move to the fountain outside again. Charles makes a joke of the situation, and Julia says she hates when he does that and hits him across the face with her switch. Twice. Then she asks if it hurt, cries, and kisses him.
- The next night Charles has to listen through Rex and his associates babbling again about current events. He and Julia escape outside to be alone.

Book Two: A Twitch Upon the Thread, Chapter Four

- Charles works out the details of his divorce with Celia's brother, Boy. She gets the kids and he pays for their education. She also gets to keep the house with her new boyfriend, Robin.
- Boy doesn't seem too upset about the divorce; he even tells Charles that he's always had a soft spot for Julia himself.
- Charles's father is disturbed that his son is getting divorced at thirty-four. He thought that they were a happy couple. Charles corrects him and explains that he's getting married again first thing.
- Mr. Ryder thinks this is stupid and advises Charles to "give up the whole idea."
- Rex adds his opinion to the pot. He thinks that if Charles wants to get divorced, fine, but he shouldn't ruin Rex's own happy marriage to Julia. He asks Charles to talk her out of wanting a divorce.
- Charles narrates that Rex's life isn't going well. He hasn't played his political cards right and there's always too much written about him in the papers.
- Even Brideshead's new woman, Beryl, puts in her two cents: every family has one lapsed Catholic, and they're usually the nicest one.
- Julia finds Beryl to be old, friendly, and bossy. Julia believes that she's exaggerating her religious nature in order to get Brideshead to marry her. Meanwhile, he is in an "amorous stupor, poor beast."
- Charles's cousin Jasper wonders why Charles is buying the cow when he can get the milk for free.
- The divorces are made final.
- In November, Charles and Julia are together at Brideshead when they are informed that Cordelia is on her way. Charles hasn't seen her for twelve years.
- Julia explains that Cordelia was in a convent for a bit, but that didn't work out. She then went to Spain to help as a nurse in the war effort. She calls her sister "odd" and adds that

Cordelia has grown up "quite plain."
- When she finally arrives, Charles believes her to now be an ugly woman, which is a shame, since she used to possess what he calls a "burning love." He wonders at how she, Brideshead, Julia, and Sebastian could all possibly be siblings.
- After dinner, the three of them go upstairs to see Nanny Hawkins. Charles recalls that, when he broke it to her about the divorces and upcoming marriage, all she said was that she hoped it was for the best. She also thinks it's about time that Brideshead got married already.
- Only now, while Charles watches Cordelia converse with her old nanny, does he realize that she (Cordelia) has her own sort of beauty.
- Cordelia announces that she saw Sebastian last month, and that now he is with the monks in Tunis.
- Nanny compares Brideshead to Sebastian, noting that the latter was never one for church and was always so beautiful and clean looking, whereas Brideshead looked ragged all the time.
- Julia has a talk with Charles. She is surprised that he has forgotten Sebastian, who was, as Charles said in the storm, "the forerunner." Julia wonders if she, too, is just a forerunner…
- Charles (internally) wonders the same thing. Maybe every love is simply a forerunner to another, he wonders. He adds that he has not forgotten Sebastian, that his friend lives daily with him in Julia, or rather Julia lived through Sebastian way back when.
- The next day, while they walk around the grounds together, Cordelia tells Charles that she heard Sebastian was dying and so went to find him. When she got to Tunis, she heard the whole story. Sebastian refused to eat despite his plentiful wealth and so was emaciated by the time he arrived at the monastery. She said he wanted to live in the bush with cannibals. Or lepers. But he didn't want any training at being a missionary or anything. The Superior told him he needed a missionary himself; Sebastian agreed and left.
- But he kept coming back to the monastery, drunk, several times a week. Cordelia explains to Charles that the Superior was a very holy man and could sense this holiness in Sebastian, which is why he tolerated him. Charles is at a loss to understand any sort of holiness in his friend.
- Anyway, Sebastian got so ill from not eating and drinking too much that the monastery had to take him in.
- When Cordelia arrived, Sebastian explained that Kurt had been very sick, and that he took him to Greece to get better. Somehow or another Kurt was arrested and hauled back to Germany, which left Sebastian alone again.
- Or not. Sebastian chased after Kurt, but found him newly reformed and a member of Hitler's growing regime. That lasted about five minutes before he admitted he hated Germany and tried to skip town with Sebastian again. Kurt was caught and thrown in a concentration camp, where he hanged himself.
- Sebastian continued to drink alone until he decided to live amongst the savages, which is how he ended up in Tunis. She says that she and Sebastian are similar in that they don't fit in either to the real world or the monastic rule.
- In their stroll about the Brideshead estate, Charles and Cordelia come to a bridge. She says that she had a governess who once jumped off and drowned herself. Charles says he knows this, that it's the first thing he ever heard about Cordelia.
- He asks if she told Julia all this about her brother. Most of it, she answers, but adds that

Julia never loved him the way she and Charles do.

- Cordelia envisions Sebastian living out his days as an alcoholic yet repentant part of the monastery abroad. "It's not such a bad way of getting through one's life," she says.
- She agrees with Charles's assessment that he is indeed suffering (from his alcoholism), but asserts that "no one is ever holy without suffering."
- Cordelia asks if Charles thought she was "thwarted" when he saw her for the first time after so many years. He says yes, and she responds that she thought the same thing about him and Julia.
- At dinner that night, Charles finds himself staring at Julia, "unable to turn away for love of her beauty." He decides that Julia regained what first drew him to her that night on the ship, the "store of magical sadness" that seems to say, "Surely I was made for some other purpose than this?"
- As the evening draws to a close, Charles has in mind the image of an ice fisher, warm and content inside his hut, soon to be eradicated by an avalanche rolling towards him.

Book Two: A Twitch Upon the Thread, Chapter Five

- Everyone is in the middle of divorcing or, in Brideshead's case, getting married, and changing estates when Lord Marchmain announces that he's returning to England to spend his final years at Brideshead.
- Plender, Lord Marchmain's valet in Venice, arrives a few days before his master. They make arrangements so that both he and Wilcox, the Brideshead butler, have positions.
- When Lord Marchmain arrives, he has to be lifted out of the car and helped to his feet. Cara, his mistress, has traveled with him from Italy. It's clear that he is very sick.
- Once inside, Lord Marchmain sits and insists on taking another pill, though Cara is reluctant to give him one.
- He asks that the servants make up a bedroom for him on the ground floor, since he's too ill to be traveling up the stairs to his former rooms. He tells the servants to use the Chinese drawing-room and the "Queen's bed." Charles wonders if he planned this culmination of "adult grandeur" on the way to Brideshead.
- Lord Marchmain sits with Cara, Julia, Cordelia, and Charles while the servants move around the furniture needed to make up his new bedroom. He tells them that he met Brideshead's new wife and found her "deplorable." He's horrified that his son married such a woman.
- He speaks of the upcoming war (this is 1939) and speculates on what will happen to all of them. Charles comments that he's negotiating for a position on the Special Reserve, and Lord Marchmain callously remarks about having an artist (like Charles) with his squadron during the war...until he died.
- Charles is surprised by this new attitude.
- Lord Marchmain looks at his new bedroom and remarks that Charles should paint it and title it "The Death Bed."
- Cara later confirms that, yes, Lord Marchmain is dying, of some disease of the heart.
- They all have dinner together in the recently made-up bedroom with Lord Marchmain.
- At bedtime, he asks Cordelia to sit with him until he falls asleep. She later remarks that she

thinks he is afraid of the dark.
- Another night, Lord Marchmain again discusses his dislike for Beryl, Brideshead's new wife. He doesn't want her to become chatelaine at Brideshead. As such, he's decided to leave the entire estate to Julia and Charles, rather than to his eldest son as expected.
- Julia tries to protest, but he insists that she is so beautiful that she belongs in the beautiful estate.
- Julia and Charles discuss the matter later, privately. Julia says she plans to accept the offer of the estate, since her brother and Beryl would be happier someplace smaller anyway.
- In retrospect and through the narration, Charles admits that he was tempted by the offer, that he was captured again by the vision he had when he first discovered the estate alongside Sebastian. Brideshead seems to him a world of art and beauty, separate from the rest of reality.
- Weeks pass. Lord Marchmain can never bear to be alone and insists that his children keep him company always.
- Brideshead and Beryl come to visit, but Lord Marchmain doesn't want to be around them. Charles feels a bit guilty around Julia's brother, knowing as he does that he will get Brideshead's inheritance.
- Realizing that they are not wanted, Brideshead and Beryl leave.
- More time passes, and Lord Marchmain remains essentially bed-ridden.
- At Easter, 3-4 months since he first arrived, Lord Marchmain gets sicker. Brideshead is summoned back to the estate, this time alone, and concludes that his father must see a priest.
- Charles is angry. It's clear that, for all of Lord Marchmain's life, he has hated religion. Charles finds it deplorable that his family would try to sic a priest on Lord Marchmain when his mind is too weak to resist.
- Julia lashes out at Charles when he voices these concerns to her. He has the sense that "the fate of more souls than one" depend on this visit from the priest.
- Finally, Father Mackay is brought to Brideshead – but Lord Marchmain refuses to speak with him. Charles feels triumphant. The "thread" which has hung over him and Julia has been averted, he feels. He also revels in the knowledge that Brideshead has likely ticked off his father even more and is farther from his inheritance than ever.
- That night, Charles and Cara ask about the details of the Last Sacrament which Brideshead and Cordelia are so intent on their father having. They all debate the nitty-gritty details of going to hell.
- Later, Julia chastises Charles for starting the argument in the first place.
- More time passes. Charles's divorce is finished and Celia marries someone else. Now he and Julia are waiting for September, when Julia's divorce will be final and they can get married at last.
- Charles is put on the "in case of emergency" list with the War Office.
- Speaking with one of Lord Marchmain's doctors one day, Charles remarks that the old man has an incredible will to live. The doctor counters that it's actually the fear of death keeping Lord Marchmain alive.
- Either way, Lord Marchmain refuses to be left alone. He wants to talk all the time. Charles provides a few pages of the sort of rambling Lord Marchmain gives in his final days. He seems to be deteriorating mentally. It also seems as though he feels guilty about the way he treated his wife (leaving her alone and moving to Italy with a mistress).

- In July, while Cordelia is out of town, Lord Marchmain's condition worsens. Julia goes to get the priest.
- After she leaves, Charles wants the doctor to help him "stop this nonsense" with religion. The doctor replies that it is not his concern, though he admits that the shock of seeing the priest will likely kill Lord Marchmain.
- When Julia returns with the priest, Charles tries to get Cara on his side against them. Tensions rise.
- After a brief argument, they all go into the room with the priest. He begins to pray, and Charles kneels and prays with them. While Father Mackay asks for a sign from Lord Marchmain that he understands, Charles hopes (silently) that the dying man will comply, if only for the sake of Julia.
- Lord Marchmain does indeed make the sign of the cross, and the little ceremony is over.
- Outside, as they wait for the car to drive Father Mackay home, Charles gives him a three-pound donation.
- Julia remains inside by her father's side, and Lord Marchmain passes away that evening.
- Charles now recalls the last words between him and Julia.
- Later that night, they are finally alone. Both of them know without saying it directly that their relationship is over. Charles says he's known for some time now, but Julia says she only just realized it.
- Julia tries to apologize and explain. Charles says he gets it, and wants to know what she's going to do with her life.
- Julia says that the more she pushes away God, the more she needs Him. She worries that starting a life with Charles would mean a life without God. There is one thing unforgivable, she says, and today she realized she might do it: "set up a rival good to God's." She feels she needs to give up this one good thing – a life with Charles happily ever after at Brideshead – in order for God to forgive her for all the wrong she has done.
- Charles says he hopes Julia's heart will break, but that he understands.
- In narration, Charles returns to his prior vision of the ice fisher, now buried under the avalanche.

Epilogue

- We return to our frame story, where Charles and his fellow officers are camping out at the Brideshead estate during WWII.
- The commanding officer calls it "the worst place [they've] struck yet" because of the lack of amenities. When he asks if anyone knows the area, Charles says nothing.
- Shortly after, a lieutenant-colonel takes Charles around the castle. He narrates that it belongs to a Lady Julia Flyte, who used to be married to Rex something-or-other. She's abroad. He finds it odd that the old Marquis left everything to his daughter, and that this decision was "rough on the boys" (likely meaning it was hard for Lord Marchmain's sons to accept).
- As he shows Charles around the different rooms, he mentions the rather modern paintings on the walls that the soldiers have mostly destroyed while lodging there. (These, of course, are Charles's paintings.)

- The lieutenant-colonel points out the Chinese drawing-room and the fountain outside, which he knows to have great sentimental value to Lady Julia. He throws a cigarette into the empty fountain before leaving Charles.
- Charles then explores the castle alone. He runs into the old housemaid who recognizes him and points him upstairs to Nanny Hawkins.
- Nanny explains to Charles what's happened in the last few years. Brideshead and Beryl kept getting turned out of their place of residence by the military. Mr. Mottram is doing very well politically and financially. Julia and Cordelia are together abroad, helping with the war effort in what Nanny believes to be Palestine, where Brideshead is as well with his yeomanry.
- After speaking with Nanny Hawkins, Charles leaves and finds Hooper, who asks if Charles knows this place.
- Charles responds that yes, he does, that it belongs to friends of his. He remembers asking Sebastian the same thing so many years ago, and Sebastian answering that it was the place where his family lives.
- Hooper finds it wasteful that such a large place was built for just one family.
- Charles responds that buildings are built for a strict purpose. He imagines it's much like having a son and wondering how he'll grow up.
- Then he adds: "I don't know; I never built anything, and I forfeited the right to watch my son grow up. I'm homeless, childless, middle-aged, loveless."
- Hooper decides to take this as a joke, and laughs.
- Charles then heads, alone, to the one part of Brideshead he hasn't yet revisited: the chapel. He finds that it looks as bright and new as ever, and that a lamp is still burning before the altar. He says a prayer and leaves.
- Charles reflects on the men who originally built Brideshead and all the architectural changes it went through throughout the years. He feels that all that work has been "brought to nothing," and reflects on the line *quomodo sedet sola civitas*. (Remember, this means "How the city sits alone" and is followed by "which was once filled by people." You heard this line the first time at the end of Book I, when Cordelia quotes it to Charles.)
- Charles then cites another religious saying, "Vanity of vanities, all is vanity." Yet Charles feels this is "a dead word from ten years back."
- Charles feels that something unintended came from all the work of the builders and out of the "small tragedy" in which he took part: the "small red flame" burning inside the terribly-designed art-nouveau lamp before the tabernacle on the altar. Charles is renewed by this discovery, convinced that such a flame burns for everyone, and that it could have been lit again "only for the builders and the tragedians."
- He quickens his pace and walks back to the hut, where the second-in-command remarks that he is looking "unusually cheerful today."

Themes

Theme of Friendship

Brideshead Revisited revolves around a close friendship between two young men who meet in college. Loyalty is tested when friendship comes in conflict with family, and a territorial sense of ownership means tensions run high. The relationship between these young men or may not be sexual in nature, but it is undeniably one of unconditional love. Friendship is an isolating force in this novel; the closer the two young men become, the less they care to interact with the rest of the world. And the more the world impinges on their time together, the further they are driven apart.

Questions About Friendship

1. Sebastian declares that he is friends with Kurt because "it's a rather pleasant change when all your life you've had people looking after you, to have someone to look after yourself." Does this also explain his affinity for Charles?
2. You've heard our two cents on the matter, but how do *you* interpret Charles and Sebastian's relationship? Do you think there is romantic love involved? Sexual love? Specifically, what passages in the text help to interpret this?
3. Does Charles abandon Sebastian, or does Sebastian abandon Charles?

Chew on Friendship

Charles and Sebastian's friendship is only possible in isolation from the rest of the world.

Charles and Sebastian's friendship is predicated upon mutual deception.

Theme of Religion

Catholicism is a main focus of *Brideshead Revisited*. From hurried pre-wedding conversions to dinner-table debates on dogma, religion dominates the novel's thematic focus. Every character struggles with religion in one way or another, even the agnostic central character. The one concept everyone seems to agree on is that to be holy is to suffer. In accordance with this principle, the most religious characters in the novel choose to suffer to be closer to God. Waugh explained that his intention was for every character to accept divine grace in his own way, though critics disagree on whether the novel ultimately reads for or against Catholicism.

Questions About Religion

1. Sebastian claims he believes in religion because it is "a lovely idea." Why does Julia base her faith on?
2. Why is Charles so adamantly against Lord Marchmain having a priest at his death? He says that the answer to this question is "unformed" but laying "in a pocket of [his] mind"…what is this getting at? Does he ever answer it for Julia? For himself?

3. Julia believes one has to sacrifice happiness to be close to God. Sebastian seems to have done the same thing. But what does Charles willingly do in the way of sacrifice? What explains his apparent piety at the end of the novel?
4. Charles tells Brideshead that, without religion, Sebastian might have had a chance to be happy. Cordelia in a way affirms this when she says that Sebastian is very holy, and no one is ever holy without suffering. If Cordelia is right, and one does need to suffer to be close to God, why do the characters in this novel choose to be religious? What's the up side?

Chew on Religion

Religion tore Sebastian and Charles apart, yet drove Julia and Charles together.

Religion prevents Charles from ever being close to any of the Flyte children.

Theme of Family

Family is a huge source of conflict in *Brideshead Revisited*. The novel takes place in England over the course of the 1920s and '30s, when rank and titles among the aristocracy meant that expectations were high and obligations strict; men were expected to act as the head of estates and women to marry a suitable match. Family is also the source of much of the religious conflict in the novel, since children are raised according to their mother's religion. More than one essentially forced conversion goes down within the course of the narrative, and always in the name of marriage and family.

Questions About Family

1. It seems that Charles's father and Sebastian's father could not be more different, especially when it comes to their relationships with their sons. So what do you make of the fact that the word "poppet" is used to describe *both* men?
2. Charles wonders at how "the same ingredients" could produce Julia, Sebastian, Brideshead, and Cordelia. Besides their shared religious, aristocratic upbringing, what do these siblings have in common?
3. Why didn't Lord Marchmain come back to England right after his wife died? Why does he choose (eventually) to die at Brideshead?

Chew on Family

Family is a purely negative influence in *Brideshead Revisited*.

Charles seeks a replacement family by becoming part of the Flytes.

Theme of Memory and The Past

Brideshead Revisited is told as a first-person narrative by a middle-aged man recalling what, for him, were much better days: his college years at Oxford and the decade that followed. While his memories are laced with the bitter melancholy of nostalgia, the act of remembering is ultimately a positive one. The narrator learns from his recollection and, despite the sad and destructive end to his story, is enlightened and buoyed by the process.

Questions About Memory and The Past

1. How honest is narrator Charles about the actions and feelings of his younger self?
2. How does Charles view the past? With bitterness? Nostalgia? Regret?
3. Does it seem from his narration that Charles has forgiven Julia for leaving him?

Chew on Memory and The Past

It is only through the process of recollection – through *revisiting* Brideshead and everything it represents to him – that Charles is able come to peace with his past and end the novel on an optimistic note.

Theme of Youth

Youth is repeatedly referred to as "Arcadia," or heaven, in *Brideshead Revisited*. The novel is told as the recollection of a middle-aged man, so it may well be that a pair of rose-colored glasses is tainting the vision. Nevertheless, youth is presented in all the hazy splendor of a lovely, eternal dream. From lazy days drinking champagne to long strolls in gardens to narrator's first, eye-opening introduction to a world of art and architecture, there's little to dislike in this Arcadian paradise.

Questions About Youth

1. Is "Arcadia" the right term for Charles's summer at Brideshead with Sebastian? Or is this a rose-colored glasses thing for the middle-aged Captain of infantry, as he calls himself?
2. Speaking of, Charles again refers to his age in the novel's epilogue, when he calls himself "homeless, child-less, middle-aged, loveless." Is it his age that upsets him so much, or his circumstance?
3. While Charles is in South America, he claims that he "remained unchanged, still a small part of [him] pretending to be whole." What makes him feel incomplete? What is he missing and what does he need in order to be whole?

Chew on Youth

Charles and Sebastian's friendship was dependent on youth and could not exist once they both became adults.

Theme of Art and Culture

Brideshead Revisited is the story of a young man's aesthetic education as he discovers a world of architectural beauty and struggles to build a life as an artist. Nearly all the novel's main relationships revolve around aesthetics, from love affairs based on beauty to friendships based on friendships built solely around artistic instruction. One idea explored in the novel is the threat of charm to artistic sensibilities. British charm in particular, claims one aesthete, is deadly, as it will strangle artistic passion by keeping it all neat and orderly.

Questions About Art and Culture

1. Trace Charles's aesthetic growth throughout the novel. What does he learn, when, and from whom?
2. Who is the greater influence on Charles's artistry – Sebastian or Anthony? What do they each do for Charles? What about Celia – does she encourage or stifle his abilities?
3. How much of Charles's love for Julia has to do with her beauty? For that matter, how much of his friendship with Sebastian is based on his "epicene beauty"?
4. Charles finds Julia's sadness to be "the completion of her beauty." What kind of connection is THAT? Why would being sad and wondering if her life holds any value make her more beautiful? Weird

Chew on Art and Culture

In *Brideshead Revisited*, Charles finds God through art.

Through his novel, Waugh condemns Charles's attempt to replace God with art.

Theme of Drugs and Alcohol

Alcoholism is at the center of *Brideshead Revisited* and essentially destroys a beautiful, charming young man. Of course, the alcoholism itself is driven by a slew of other problems, namely family and religion. The young man in question turns to the substance as a means of escaping, retreating further and further into self-imposed isolation by means of intense bouts of drinking. As is said many times in the novel, alcohol is used primarily as an escape.

Questions About Drugs and Alcohol

1. Which is the greater cause of Sebastian's drinking problem – his family, or his religion? Does Charles identify it as one or the other?
2. According to the Flytes' Catholicism, can Sebastian be holy *and* an alcoholic? What about the whole "to be holy is to suffer" thing – how does that factor in here?
3. In "Character Analysis," we theorize that Cordelia and Charles are the only two characters to really love Sebastian. If we're right, why is it that these are the only two to sneak Sebastian booze while everyone else is trying to cure him of his alcoholism?

Chew on Drugs and Alcohol

Each character's love for Sebastian is tested – and either proved or disproved – through his or her reaction to his alcoholism.

Theme of Society and Class

Brideshead Revisited offers a view into the world of British aristocracy in the 1920s and '30s. Titles, rank, and the obligations that go with them threaten to determine the course of each character's life. Wealth in particular is a focus of the novel, especially the vulgar extravagance of the British upper class which is repeatedly compared to the natural beauty of places like Morocco, Tunis, or South America.

Questions About Society and Class

1. What does Charles learn when he goes off into the jungles of South America? About art? About British aristocracy?
2. Anthony warns Charles that British charm will ruin him and his artistry. Does it? What do you think of Anthony's assessment of Charles's work – the work which everyone else finds so "virile" and "passionate?" Does Charles agree with Anthony's criticism?
3. How is British aristocracy portrayed in this novel? Waugh certainly pokes fun at it – think about the diamond-studded tortoise or the life-size swan carving filled with caviar – but does that mean he's egalitarian? (Most critics say "no," and in fact claim it's just the opposite; how can you use the text to justify this common interpretation?)

Chew on Society and Class

Lady Marchmain uses religion to mask her classist discriminations.

Theme of Love

The narrator of *Brideshead Revisited* struggles to understand and define love over the course of two decades. The novel explores many different kinds of love, from the "romantic" but not necessarily sexual love between young men to sexual relationships between men to stilted marriages to sibling relationships. One unique perspective the novel offers is the idea of a first and second love: boys experience this first love shortly before they become men. It is an immature forerunner to the mature, complete love he will experience next. By the end of the novel, however, even this has been called into question, as the narrator wonders if perhaps *all* loves are simply a forerunner to the next, ad infinitum…

Questions About Love

1. It's pretty clear that Charles in no way loves his wife once he gets back from South America. (See "Character Analysis" for more detail.) Has he fallen victim to the same problem of a first love that Cara claimed plagued Lord Marchmain's marriage? Or was Sebastian Charles's problematic first love?
2. After Charles and Julia have finalized their divorces and are planning to marry, Cordelia

describes their relationship with the words "thwarted passion." What does she mean by this? IS their relationship thwarted? If so, what is responsible for the thwarting – religion? Family? How could Cordelia, who has seen them for about two minutes after many absent years, conclude this so quickly?

3. Charles tells Julia that Sebastian was the forerunner to their love. He wonders if Sebastian is with him, through Julia, or if Julia was with him through Sebastian. Whom does he actually love, and who is just his way of getting closer to the other?

Chew on Love
Charles loves Julia as a piece of beautiful art, not as a person.

In *Brideshead Revisited*, love is essentially the ability to communicate honestly.

Friendship Quotes
"You may think it charming. I think it's devilish. Do you know he spent the whole of yesterday evening trying to turn me against you, and almost succeeded?"

"Did he? How silly. Aloysius wouldn't approve of that at all, would you, you pompous old bear?" (1.2.78-9)

Thought: This is a brilliantly constructed conclusion to the conversation with Anthony. Just as we are inclined to believe Sebastian and write off Anthony's warning, Sebastian does exactly as Anthony predicted.

"Oh, Mummy likes everything to be a present. She's so sweet," he said, adding one more line to the picture I was forming of her.

Now Sebastian had disappeared into that other life of hi where I was not asked to follow, and I was left, instead, forlorn and regretful. (1.3.4-5)

Thought: Charles is left alone because, not having much of a family himself, he can't understand what Sebastian is dealing with in regards to Lady Marchmain. The same thing happens with religion – the barrier of misunderstanding separates these two friends.

I saw, in my mind's eye, the pale face of Anthony Blanche, peering through the straggling leaves as it had peered through the candle flames at Thame, and heard, above the murmur of traffic, his clear tones [...] "You mustn't blame Sebastian if at times he seems a little insipid. [...] When I hear him talk I am reminded of that in some ways nauseating picture of 'Bubbles.' [...] Boredom [...] like a cancer in the breast [...]"

For days after that I thought I hated Sebastian. (1.3.94-5)

Thought: Charles recognizes that Anthony is right – Sebastian *is* in many ways insipid – but he loves him for it anyway. He has no illusions about his friend, but rather accepts him as he is.

"We'll have a heavenly time alone," said Sebastian, and when next morning, while I was shaving, I saw from my bathroom window Julia, with luggage at her back, drive from the forecourt and disappear at the hill's crest, without a backward glance, I felt a sense of liberation and peace such as I was to know years-later when, after a night of unrest, the sirens sounded the All Clear. (1.3.144)

Thought: Charles and Sebastian's friendship can only exist peacefully as long they are isolated from the rest of the world.

"I think you are very fond of Sebastian," she said.

"Why, certainly."

"I know of these romantic friendships of the English and the Germans. They are not Latin. I think they are very good if they do not go on too long." (1.4.101)

Thought: Cara essentially puts an expiration date on Charles and Sebastian's friendship – and she's right. In many ways, their relationship is a very childish one, and cannot possibly be expected to hold up to the trials of adulthood.

It was thus that Lady Marchmain found us when, early in that Michaelmas term, she came for a week to Oxford. She found Sebastian subdued, with all his host of friends reduced to one, myself. She accepted me as Sebastian's friend and sought to make me hers also, and in doing so, unwittingly struck at the roots of our friendship. That is the single reproach I have to set against her abundant kindness to me. (1.5.27)

Thought: Cara discusses how Lord Marchmain hated Lady Marchmain and so despised anyone close to her. The same goes for Sebastian, though his hate is less extreme and definitely hidden. He can't be friends with Charles if Charles is friends with his mother.

I had seen him grow wary at the thought of his family or his religion; now I found I, too, was suspect. He did not fail in love, but he lost his joy of it, for I was no longer part of his solitude. As my intimacy with his family grew I became part of the world which he sought to escape; I became one of the bonds which held him. (1.5.206)

Thought: This makes us wonder what drew Sebastian to Charles in the first place – was it just a way of escaping his family by forming a close bond with someone else to replace them?

"Did you have a 'little talk' with Mummy?"

"Yes."

"Have you gone over to her side?"

The day before I would have said: "There aren't two sides"; that day I said, "No, I'm with you, Sebastian contra mundum."

And that was all the conversation we had on the subject, then or ever. (1.5.333-7)

Thought: This is the defining moment in Charles's relationship with Sebastian; *contra mundum* is the only type of friendship Sebastian is willing to have (or even capable of having).

It was repugnant to me to talk about Sebastian to Mr. Samgrass. (1.6.119)

Thought: Once he commits to the friendship, Charles is fiercely loyal to his friend.

Poor simple monk, I thought, poor booby; but he added, "You know why? He has a bottle of cognac in bed with him. It is the second I have found. No sooner do I take one away than he gets another. He is so naughty. It is the Arab boys who fetch it for him. But it is good to see him happy again when he has been so sad." (1.8.133)

Thought: Charles recognizes that Sebastian has completely duped the monk, but he doesn't judge him for it. Those who really love Sebastian – namely Charles and Cordelia – love him unconditionally, including the alcoholism. He's a whole package deal, and Charles takes him as he is.

"You know, Charles," he said, "it's rather a pleasant change when all your life you've had people looking after you, to have someone to look after yourself. Only of course it has to be someone pretty hopeless to need looking after by me." (1.8.136)

Thought: Who takes care of whom in the Charles/Sebastian relationship?

Religion Quotes

"He and I were both Catholics, so we used to go to mass together. He used to spend such a time in the confessional, I used to wonder what he had to say, because he never did anything wrong; never quite; at least, he never got punished. Perhaps he was just being charming

through the grille." (1.2.38)

Thought: Anthony has little or no understanding of Catholicism as Sebastian understands it and as Charles will come to understand it by the end of the novel.

Often, almost daily, since I had known Sebastian, some chance word in his conversation had reminded me that he was a Catholic, but I took it as a foible, like his Teddy-bear. We never discussed the matter until on the second Sunday at Brideshead, when Father Phipps had left us and we sat in the colonnade with the papers, he surprised me by saying: "Oh dear, it's very difficult being a Catholic." (1.4.50)

Thought: Sebastian struggles with Catholicism because he takes it so seriously. Charles, who finds the whole thing (at this point in his flashback) to be somewhat ridiculous, can't understand this.

"I mean about Christmas and the star and the three kings and the ox and the ass."

"Oh yes, I believe that. It's a lovely idea."

"But you can't believe things because they're a lovely idea."

"But I do. That's how I believe." (1.4.63-66)

Thought: Sebastian is the ultimate aesthete – even his religious beliefs are based on beauty.

"Well," I said, "if you can believe all that and you don't want to be good, where's the difficulty about your religion?"

"If you can't see, you can't." (1.4.69-70)

Thought: At what point in the novel *does* Charles begin to see this?

"Cordelia has promised to pray for me," I said.

"She made a novena for her pig," said Sebastian.

"You know all this is very puzzling to me," I said.

"I think we're causing scandal," said Brideshead.

That night I began to realize how little I really knew of Sebastian, and to understand why he had always sought to keep me apart from the rest of his life. He was like a friend made on board ship, on the high seas; now we had come to his home port. (1.4.156-160)

Thought: Charles earlier commented that, when discussing his family, Sebastian would retreat into another world where Charles could not follow. It seems now that religion is largely responsible for this rift between the two young men.

"When people hate with all that energy, it is something in themselves they are hating. Alex is hating all the illusions of boyhood – innocence, God, hope. Poor Lady Marchmain has to bear all that." (1.4.236)

Thought: Here Cara is trying to explain why everyone hates Lady Marchmain. Cordelia later continues this discussion when she says that people hate Lady Marchmain as an indirect way of hating God.

Between her tears she talked herself into silence. I could do nothing; I was adrift in a strange sea; my hands on the metal-spun threads of her tunic were cold and stiff, my eyes dry; I was as far from her in spirit, as she clung to me in the darkness, as when years ago I had lit her cigarette on the way from the station; as far as when she was out of mind, in the dry, empty years at the Old Rectory and in the jungle. (2.3.119)

Thought: Just as religion was the barrier between Charles and Sebastian, so it is here between him and Julia – not because he resents her for her beliefs, but because he simply cannot understand them.

"There were four of you," I said. "Cara didn't know the first thing it was about, and may or may not have believed it; you knew a bit and didn't believe a word; Cordelia knew about as much and believed it madly; only poor Bridey knew and believed, and I thought he made a pretty poor show when it came to explaining. And people go round saying, 'At least Catholics know what they believe.' We had a fair cross-section to-night–"

"Oh, Charles, don't rant. I shall begin to think you're getting doubts yourself." (2.5.161-2)

Thought: Actually, Julia is right – Charles is beginning to doubt his own doubt. We know that he has found God by the end of the novel, so this is the first inkling of his eventual conversion.

"That is what it would mean; starting a life with you, without Him. […] But I saw to-day there was one thing unforgivable – like things in the schoolroom, so bad they are unpunishable, that only Mummy could deal with – the bad thing I was on the point of doing, that I'm not quite bad enough to do; to set up a rival good to God's. […] It may be a private bargain between me and God, that if I give up this one thing I want so much, however bad I am, He won't quite despair of me in the end." (2.5.247)

Thought: Is this really Julia's reason for leaving Charles? Or is she justifying? Are the barriers she faces religious, or simply social taboos?

Family Quotes

"You must see the garden front and the fountain." He leaned forward and put the car into gear. "It's where my family live." And even then, rapt in the vision, I felt, momentarily, like a wind stirring the tapestry, an ominous chill at the words he used – not "That is my home," but "It's where my family live." (1.1.83)

Thought: Sebastian feels distant and separated from Brideshead because he so resents his family. He can never appreciate the estate the way Charles comes to.

"I'm not going to have you get mixed up with my family. They're so madly charming. All my life they've been taking things away from me. If they once got hold of you with their charm, they'd make you their friend, not mine, and I won't let them." (1.1.106)

Thought: Remember what Anthony later says about charm? Interestingly, Sebastian says his family manipulates with charm, whereas Anthony claims Sebastian does this very same thing.

"Perhaps I am rather curious about people's families – you see, it's not a thing I know about. There is only my father and myself. An aunt kept an eye on me for a time but my father drove her abroad. My mother was killed in the war." (1.1.128)

Thought: We expect Charles to be drawn to Lady Marchmain as a replacement for his own mother.

"It's odd because there's really no mystery about him except how he came to be born of such a very sinister family.

"I forget if you know his family. Now there, my dear, is a subject for the poet – for the poet of the future who must be also a psychoanalyst – and perhaps a diabolist, too. I don't suppose he'll ever let you meet them. He's far too clever. They're all charming, of course, and quite, quite gruesome. Do you ever feel is something a teeny bit gruesome about Sebastian? No? Perhaps I imagine it; it's simply that he looks so like the rest of them, sometimes." (1.2.43-4)

Thought: Charles, too, will pick up on the physical similarities between the Flytes – in particular Julia and Sebastian. But does this reflect a deeper commonality?

"Well, I'm the worst person to come to for advice. I've never been 'short,' as you so painfully call it. And yet what else could you say? Hard up? Penurious? Distressed? Embarrassed? Stony-broke?" […] I had not seen my father so gleeful since he found two pages of

second-century papyrus between the leaves of a Lombardic breviary. [...] For the rest of dinner he was silent save for an occasional snuffle of merriment which could not, I thought, be provoked by the work he read. (1.3.23-8)

Thought: Charles's father is the epitome of callous sarcasm, yet he never ends up causing Charles the damage that Sebastian's seemingly charming family does.

It was largely by reason of my Aunt Philippa that I now found myself so much a stranger in my father's house. After my mother's death she came to live with my father and me, no doubt, as he said, with the idea of making her home with us. I knew nothing, then, of the nightly agonies at the dinner table. [...] Then in my last year at school she left England."I got her out in the end" he said with derision and triumph of that kindly lady, and he knew that I heard in the words a challenge to myself. (1.3.50)

Thought: Mr. Ryder wants nothing but to be left alone. Family is as much of a burden to him as it is to Sebastian.

He kissed Lord Marchmain on the cheek and I, who had not kissed my father since I left the nursery, stood shyly behind him. (1.4.193)

Thought: Mr. Ryder and Lord Marchmain are constantly contrasted with each other in the novel, as are their respective relationships with their sons.

Sebastian began to weep. "Why do you take their side against me? I knew you would if I let you meet them. Why do you spy on me?"

He said more than I can bear to remember, even at twenty years' distance. At last I got him to sleep and very sadly went to bed myself. (1.5.276-7)

Thought: Charles is again torn between his desire to help the Flytes deal with Sebastian's alcoholism and his desire to see his friend happy.

She had a copy lying ready on her bureau. I thought at the time, "She planned this parting before ever I came in. Had she rehearsed all the interview? If things had gone differently would she have put the book back in the drawer?" (1.5.321)

Thought: Sebastian's distrust of his mother proves warranted here. It is not until Charles realizes her intentions that he agrees to side with Sebastian, "contra mundum."

"Then you agree to my leaving Oxford?"

"Agree? Agree? My dear boy, you're twenty-two."

"Twenty," I said, "twenty-one in October."

"Is that all? It seems much longer." (1.5.437-40)

Thought: Compare Charles's interaction with his father to Sebastian's relationship with his family. Charles is left to fend for himself while Sebastian's family babies him to death – they are likely responsible for his refusal to leave childhood behind.

Memory and The Past Quotes

He told me and, on the instant, it was as though someone had switched off the wireless, and a voice that had been bawling in my ears, incessantly, fatuously, for days beyond number, had been suddenly cut short; an immense silence followed, empty at first, but gradually, as my outraged sense regained authority, full of a multitude of sweet and natural and long-forgotten sounds – for he had spoken a name that was so familiar to me, a conjuror's name of such ancient power, that, at its mere sound, the phantoms of those haunted late years began to take flight. (prologue.95)

Thought: It seems that Charles has shut away the past and moved on completely from Brideshead and the Flyte family. Revisiting the estate, then, is more than just a trip down memory lane – he's forced to deal with the past that he has shut away.

"Just the place to bury a crock of gold," said Sebastian. "I should like to bury something precious in every place where I've been happy and then, when I was old and ugly and miserable, I could come back and dig it up and remember." (1.1.20)

Thought: Indeed, Charles "digs up" this idea again, towards the end of Book One, Chapter Six. He drives away from Brideshead and feels he will return again "as ghosts are said to do, frequenting the spots where they buried material treasures." Interesting…

It is easy, retrospectively, to endow one's youth with a false precocity or a false innocence; to tamper with the dates marking one's stature on the edge of the door. I should like to think – indeed I sometimes do think – that I decorated those rooms with Morris stuffs and Arundel prints and that my shelves were filled with seventeenth-century folios and French novels of the second empire in Russia-leather and watered-silk. But this was not the truth. (1.1.28)

Thought: Charles admits the embarrassing "truth" here about the artistic preferences of his youth – but can we trust him elsewhere in his narration?

That luncheon party – for party it proved to be – was the beginning of a new epoch in my life, but its details are dimmed for me and confused by so many others, almost identical with it, that succeeded one another that term and the next, like romping cupids in a Renaissance frieze. (1.1.49)

Thought: Charles always admits the ambiguity of memory in his narrative. It's interesting to see which details he so vividly remembers and which are blurry in his mind.

I was unmoved; there was no part of me remotely touched by her distress. It was as I had often imagined being expelled from school. I almost expected to hear her say: "I have already written to inform your unhappy father." But as I drove away and turned back in the car to take what promised to be my last view of the house, I felt that I was leaving part of myself behind, and that wherever I went afterwards I should feel the lack of it, and search for it hopelessly, as ghosts are said to do, frequenting the spots where they buried material treasures without which they cannot pay their way to the nether world. (1.6.214)

Thought: Does Charles in fact find this buried part of himself when he revisits Brideshead as the Captain of infantry?

So I set out after dinner, with the consular porter going ahead, lantern in hand. Morocco was a new and strange country to me. Driving that day, mile after mile, up the smooth, strategic road, past the vineyards and military posts and the new, white settlements and the early crops already standing high in the vast, open fields, and the hoardings advertising the staples of France – Dubonnet, Michelin, Magasin du Louvre – I had thought it all very suburban and up-to-date; now, under the stars, in the walled city, whose streets were gentle, dusty stairways, and whose walls rose windowless on either side, closed overhead, then opened again to the stars; where the dust lay thick among the smooth paving stones and figures passed silently, robed in white, on soft slippers or hard, bare soles; where the air was scented with cloves and incense and wood smoke – now I knew what had drawn Sebastian here and held him so long. (1.8.88)

Thought: Charles concludes that beauty lies in the primitive and ancient, not in the charm of British modernism; this is a prelude to his trip to South America.

My theme is memory that winged host that soared above me one grey morning of war-time.

These memories, which are my life – for we possess nothing certainly except the past –, were always with me. (2.1.1-2)

Thought: Charles may be a middle-aged captain of infantry now, but he is defined by the events in his past. This may go some way in explaining his new-found optimism at the close of the novel.

It needed this voice from the past to recall me; the indiscriminate chatter of praise all that crowded day had worked on me like a succession of advertisement hoardings on a long road, kilometre after kilometre between the poplars, commanding one to stay at some new hotel, so that when at the end of the drive, stiff and dusty, one arrives at the destination, it seems inevitable to turn into the yard under the name that had first bored, then angered one, and finally become an inseparable part of one's fatigue. (2.2.50)

Thought: Charles isolates the past as a completely separate part of his life. The titular "revisit" refers not just to Brideshead, but also to his past, which he explores through his narration.

Youth Quotes

I went there uncertainly, for it was foreign ground and there was a tiny, priggish, warning voice in my ear which [...] told me it was seemly to hold back. But I was in search of love in those days, and I went full of curiosity and the faint, unrecognized apprehension that here, at last, I should find that low door in the wall, which others, I knew, had found before me, which opened on an enclosed and enchanted garden, which was somewhere, not overlooked by any window, in the heart of that grey city. (1.1.50)

Thought: Charles's fascination with Sebastian is akin to the childlike wonder of the unknown.

He was magically beautiful, with that epicene quality which in extreme youth sings aloud for love and withers at the first cold wind. (1.1.53)

Thought: Charles hints at the fragility and transience of Sebastian's beauty.

In the event, that Easter vacation formed a short stretch of level road in the precipitous descent of which Jasper warned me. Descent or ascent? It seems to me that I grew younger daily with each adult habit that I acquired. I had lived a lonely childhood [...]. Now, that summer term with Sebastian, it seemed as though I was being given a brief spell of what I had never known, a happy childhood, and though its toys were silk shirts and liqueurs and cigars and its naughtiness high in the catalogue of grave sins, there was something of nursery freshness about us that fell little short of the joy of innocence. (1.2.18)

Thought: This is what draws Charles to Sebastian: his beauty, yes, but also his *youthfulness*.

At times we all seemed children beside him – at most times, but not always, for there was a bluster and zest in Anthony which the rest of us had shed somewhere in our more leisured adolescence, on the playing field or in the school-room; his vices flourished less in the pursuit of pleasure than in the wish to shock. [...] He was competitive in the bet-you-can't-do-this style of the private school. [...] He was cruel, too, in the wanton, insect-maiming manner of the very young and 'fearless, like a little boy, charging, head down, small fists whirling, at the school prefects. (1.2.26)

Thought: It'd interesting that Charles describes Anthony as childish, when he is in fact the one to impart the most important information to Charles regarding Sebastian and Charles's own artistry. Looks like another example of the inverse relationship between wisdom and age in *Brideshead Revisited*.

How ungenerously in later life we disclaim the virtuous moods of our youth, living in retrospect long, summer days of unreflecting dissipation, Dresden figures of pastoral gaiety! Our wisdom, we prefer to think, is all of our own gathering, while, if the truth be told, it is, most of it, the last coin of a legacy that dwindles with time. There is no candour in a story of early manhood which leaves out of account the home-sickness for nursery morality, the regrets and resolutions of amendment, the black hours which, like zero on the roulette table, turn up with roughly calculable regularity. (1.3.6)

Thought: All of *Brideshead* is imbued with this sense of nostalgia for youth. Passages like this one define the novel's tone.

The languor of Youth – how unique and quintessential it is! How quickly, how irrecoverably, lost! The zest, the generous affections, the illusions, the despair, all the traditional attributes of Youth – all save this – come and go with us through life; [...] but languor – the relaxation of yet unwearied sinews, the mind sequestered and self-regarding, the sun standing still in the heavens and the earth throbbing to our own pulse – that belongs to Youth alone and dies with it. [...] I, at any rate, believed myself very near heaven, during those languid days at Brideshead. (1.4.1)

Thought: For Charles, the act of revisiting Brideshead is very much the act of revisiting his youth. The novel isn't just about this estate, but what the estate represents in Charles's past.

"Sebastian is in love with his own childhood. That will make him very unhappy. His Teddy-bear, his Nanny [...] and he is nineteen years old."(1.4.238)

Thought: Oh, that Cara. Always the fountain of wisdom. She's struck at another important point in *Brideshead Revisited* – Sebastian's obsession with his youth. However, note that while Cara condemns this quality, it is also what draws Charles to Sebastian.

"Oh, Charles, what has happened since last term? I feel so old."

"I feel middle-aged. That is infinitely worse; I believe we have had all the fun we can expect here."

We sat silent in the firelight as darkness fell.

"Anthony Blanche has gone down." (1.5.9-12)

Thought: What is the difference between being middle-aged and being old, according to Charles? Remember that he stated in the prologue that he is a "middle-aged captain of infantry" and in the epilogue refers to himself as "homeless, child-less, middle-aged, loveless."

I had left behind me – what? Youth? Adolescence? Romance? The conjuring stuff of these things, "the Young Magician's Compendium," that neat cabinet where the ebony wand had its place beside the delusive billiard balls, the penny that folded double and the feather flowers that could be drawn into a hollow candle.

"I have left behind illusion," I said to myself. "Henceforth I live in a world of three dimensions – with the aid of my five senses."

I have since learned that there is no such world; but then, as the car turned out of sight of the house, I thought it took no finding, but lay all about me at the end of the avenue. (1.6.218-20)

Thought: More evidence for our theory that Brideshead represents youth to Charles. When he leaves the estate, he enters adulthood.

"But yesterday I got a regular eye-opener. The trouble with modern education is you never know how ignorant people are. With anyone over fifty you can be fairly confident what's been taught and what's been left out. But these young people have such an intelligent, knowledgeable surface, and then the crust suddenly breaks and you look down into depths of confusion you didn't know existed." (1.7.112)

Thought: This is true; for all Charles and Sebastian's education at Oxford, they know very little about themselves or what they want.

It was really Johnjohn who made him see reason about that girl; seriously, you know, he's frightfully sharp. He must have heard Mother and me talking, because next time Boy came he said: 'Uncle Boy shan't marry horrid girl and leave Johnjohn,' and that was the very day – he settled for two thousand pounds out of court." (2.2.72)

Thought: Youth is very much tied to wisdom in *Brideshead Revisited*. Cordelia, too, was a fountain of insight as a child.

"I've never known a divorce do anyone any good."

"That's your affair and Julia's."

"Oh, Julia's set on it. What I hoped was, you might be able to talk her round. I've tried to keep out of the way as much as I could; if I've been around too much, just tell me, I shan't mind. But there's too much going on altogether at the moment, what with Bridey wanting me to clear out of the house; it's disturbing, and I've got a lot on my mind."

[...]

"If Julia insists on a divorce, I suppose she must have it," he said. "But she couldn't have chosen a worse time. Tell her to hang on a bit, Charles, there's a good fellow." (2.4.16-9)

Thought: Charles's entire group of peers all act like children, even once they are grown. They all marry and divorce as though they are changing outfits.

Art and Culture Quotes

It is easy, retrospectively, to endow one's youth with a false precocity or a false innocence; to tamper with the dates marking one's stature on the edge of the door. I should like to think – indeed I sometimes do think – that I decorated those rooms with Morris stuffs and Arundel prints and that my shelves were filled with seventeenth-century folios and French novels of the second empire in Russia-leather and watered-silk. But this was not the truth. On my first afternoon I proudly hung a reproduction of Van Gogh's "Sunflowers" over the fire and set up a screen, painted by Roger Fry with a Provencal landscape, which I had bought inexpensively when the Omega workshops were sold up. I displayed [...] most painful to recall, a porcelain figure of Polly Peachum [...]. My books were meagre and commonplace [...] and my earliest friends fitted well into this background. (1.1.28)

Thought: This is the starting point for the aesthetic education that Charles will undergo throughout the course of *Brideshead Revisited*. He describes here his taste in art in his early days at Oxford – it reflects what at the time was modern art. Of course, later in the novel, Charles agrees with Cordelia that "modern art is all bosh." Much of his growth and artistic development comes from his relationship with Sebastian and the time he spends at Brideshead.

[...] and my earliest friends fitted well into this background; they were Collins, a Wykehamist, an embryo don, a man of solid reading and childlike humour, and a small circle of college intellectuals, who maintained a middle course of culture between the flamboyant "aesthetes" and the proletarian scholars who scrambled fiercely for facts in the lodging houses of the Iffley -Road and Wellington Square. [...] but even in the earliest days [...] I felt at heart that this was not all that Oxford had to offer. (1.1.28)

Thought: Charles is looking for someone like Sebastian even before he meets him. This explains why he so eagerly delves into close friendship with the eccentric man.

Collins had exposed the fallacy of modern aesthetics to me: "...The whole argument from Significant Form stands or falls by volume. If you allow Cezanne to represent a third dimension on his two-dimensional canvas, then you must allow Landseer his gleam of loyalty in the spaniel's eye"– but it was not until Sebastian, idly turning the page of Clive Bell's Art, read: "Does anyone feel the same kind of emotion for a butterfly or a flower that he feels for a cathedral or a picture? Yes. I do," that my eyes were opened. (1.1.29)

Thought: Thus begins Charles's aesthetic education at the hands of his friend Sebastian.

I knew Sebastian by sight long before I met him. That was unavoidable for, from his first week, he was the most conspicuous man of his year by reason of his beauty, which was arresting, and his eccentricities of behaviour which seemed to know no bounds. (1.1.30)

Thought: Sebastian is very much defined by his beauty. It is a constant reminder that his importance to Charles is his ability to guide him artistically.

I took my gown and left him to his task. I still frequented the lecture room in those days, and it was after eleven when I returned to college. I found my room full of flowers; what looked like, and, in fact, was, the entire day's stock of a market-stall stood in every conceivable vessel in every part of the room. (1.1.43)

Thought: Again, look at the objects which Sebastian uses – flowers. He is always associated with nature and beauty.

"Oh, Charles, what a lot you have to learn! There's a beautiful arch there and more different kinds of ivy than I knew existed. I don't know where I should be without the Botanical Gardens."

When at length I returned to my rooms and found them exactly as I had left them that morning, I detected a jejune air that had not irked me before. What was wrong? Nothing except the golden daffodils seemed to be real. Was it the screen? I turned it face to the wall. That was better. (1.1.74-5)

Thought: Charles starts developing his artistic taste as soon as he starts hanging out with Sebastian.

"You see, my dear Charles, you are that very rare thing, An Artist. [...] I have seen those little drawings you keep hidden away in your room. They are exquisite. And you, dear Charles, if you will understand me, are not exquisite; but not at all. Artists are not exquisite. I am; Sebastian, in a kind of way, is exquisite; but the Artist is an eternal type, solid, purposeful, observant – and, beneath it all, p-p-passionate, eh, Charles?" (1.2.39)

Thought: As Anthony points out, Charles is not beautiful himself. But his role as an artist is to seek out and capture beauty. This simple passage goes a long way in explaining Charles's friendship with Sebastian, his fascination with the Brideshead estate, his eventual affair with Julia, and his career as an architectural painter.

"Oh, Charles, don't be such a tourist. What does it matter when it was built, if it's pretty?"

[...]

It was an aesthetic education to live within those walls. (1.4.10,13)

Thought: To live within those walls, yes, but also to live with Sebastian, the ultimate teacher.

"Of course, you are right really," he said. "You take art as a means not as an end. That is strict theology, but it's unusual to find an agnostic believing it." (1.4.155)

Thought: AHA! Here's our big hint to a very important point in *Brideshead Revisited: aesthetics are Charles's religion* . Read "Character Analysis" for more.

It had been the custom that on every visit to Brideshead I painted a medallion on the walls of the garden-room. The custom suited me well, for it gave me a good reason to detach myself from the rest of the party; when the house was full the garden-room became a rival to the nursery, where from time to time people took refuge to complain about the others; thus without effort I kept in touch with the gossip of the place. (1.6.125)

Thought: Every aspect of painting suits Charles's persona: the isolation, the observing, the knowing without having to engage socially.

I rejoiced in the Burgundy. How can I describe it? The Pathetic Fallacy resounds in all our praise of wine. For centuries every language has been strained to define its beauty, and has produced only wild conceits or the stock epithets of the trade. This Burgundy seemed to me, then, serene and triumphant, a reminder that the world was an older and better place than Rex knew, that mankind in its long passion had learned wisdom than his. By chance I met this same wine again, lunching with my wine merchant in St. James's Street, in the first autumn of the war; it had softened and faded in the intervening years, but it still spoke in the pure, authentic accent of its prime and, that day, as at Paillard's with Rex Mottram years before, it whispered faintly, but in the same lapidary phrase, the same words of hope. (1.6.284)

Thought: Charles finds beauty in the very thing destroying Sebastian: alcohol.

"You see Charles lives for one thing – Beauty. I think he got bored with finding it ready-made in England; he had to go and create it for himself. He wanted new worlds to conquer." (2.2.24)

Thought: And now that he's tired of finding it in South America, he's made the very beautiful Julia his next conquest.

The most influential critic, who in the past had dismissed me with a few wounding commendations, peered out at me from between his slouch hat and woolen muffler, gripped my arm, and said: "I knew you had it. I saw it there. I've been waiting for it." [...] "Ryder's is the last name would have occurred to me. They're so virile, so passionate."

[...]

I remembered the exhibition, too, for another reason; it was the week I detected my wife in adultery. (2.2.26-9)

Thought: It's interesting that Charles achieves this artistic breakthrough around the same time he begins his affair with Julia. The aesthetic and the passionate are once again brought together. Of course, both Charles's supposed achievement and his love with Julia end up "thwarted" in the end.

"I went to your first exhibition," said Anthony; "I found it – charming. There was an interior of Marchmain House, very English, very correct, but quite delicious. 'Charles has done something,' I said; 'not all he will do, not all he can do, but something.'

"Even then, my dear, I wondered a little. It seemed to me that there was something a little gentlemanly about your painting. You must remember I am not English; I cannot understand this keen zest to be well-bred. English snobbery is more macabre to me even than English morals. However, I said, 'Charles has done something delicious. What will he do next?'" (2.2.60-1)

Thought: Art and aristocracy don't mix – this is what Anthony is getting at when he said earlier that charm would strangle Charles's artistry.

Drugs and Alcohol Quotes

"No. I like and think good the end to which wine is sometimes the means – the promotion of sympathy between man and man. But in my own case it does not achieve that end, so I neither like it nor think it good for me." (1.4.133)

Thought: Brideshead once again exposes his inability to communicate effectively with others.

"Sebastian drinks too much."

"I suppose we both do."

"With you it does not matter. I have watched you together. With Sebastian it is different. He will be a drunkard if someone does not come to stop him. I have known so many. Alex was nearly a drunkard when he met me; it is in the blood. I see it in the way Sebastian drinks. It is not your way." (1.4.239-41)

Thought: Cara isn't just saying that Sebastian drinks differently than Charles – she's also telling Charles that he is nothing like his friend. Sebastian's qualities – his eccentricities, his aesthetic awareness – these are unattainable attributes for Charles.

There were two girls there, contemporaries of Julia's; they all seemed involved in the management of the ball. Mulcaster knew them of old and they, without much relish I thought, knew him. Mrs. Champion talked to Rex. Sebastian and I found ourselves drinking alone together as we always did. (1.5.58)

Thought: Sebastian and Charles base their friendship on two things: drinking, and isolation from the rest of the world.

I had no mind then for anything except Sebastian, and I saw him already as being threatened, though I did not yet know how black was the threat. His constant, despairing prayer was to be let alone. By the blue waters and rustling palm of his own mind he was happy and harmless as a Polynesian; only when the big ship dropped anchor beyond the coral reef, and the cutter beached in the lagoon, and, up the golden slope that had never known the print of a boot there trod the grim invasion of trader, administrator, missionary and tourist – only then was it time to disinter the archaic weapons of the tribe and sound the drums in the hills; or, more easily, to turn from the sunlit door and lie alone in the darkness, where the impotent, painted deities paraded the walls in vain, and cough his heart out among the rum bottles. (1.5.205)

Thought: OK, we admit it: we just put this quote here so you would all read this gorgeous metaphor again. Sigh.

It was during this term that I began to realize that Sebastian was a drunkard in quite a different sense from myself. I got drunk often, but through an excess of high spirits, in the love of the moment, and the wish to prolong and enhance it; Sebastian drank to escape. As we together grew older and more serious I drank less, he more. I found that sometimes after I had gone back to my college, he sat up late and alone, soaking. (1.5.211)

Thought: This is precisely what Cara predicted earlier in the novel. Charles and Sebastian's key differences are marked by the latter's alcoholism, and their friendship is threatened by it.

Julia used to say, "Poor Sebastian. It's something chemical in him."

That was the cant phrase of the time, derived from heaven knows what misconception of popular science. "There's something chemical between them" was used to explain the overmastering hate or love of any two people. It was the old concept of determinism in a new form. I do not believe there was anything chemical in my friend. (1.5.211-3)

Thought: Charles doesn't want to blame biology for Sebastian's alcoholism. He (correctly?) identifies Sebastian's family and religion as the source of his problem.

The Easter party at Brideshead was a bitter time, culminating in a small but unforgettably painful incident. Sebastian got very drunk before dinner in his mother's house, and thus marked the beginning of a new epoch in his melancholy record of deterioration, the first step in the flight from his family which brought him to ruin. (1.5.214)

Thought: Charles reveals information about Sebastian's alcoholism as he slowly becomes aware of its causes. He earlier said that Sebastian drank to escape – now he has clarified his point further: Sebastian drinks to escape *his family.*

"No," said Brideshead, "I don't suppose you could. I once saw my father drunk, in this room. I wasn't more than about ten at the time. You can't stop people if they want to get drunk. My mother couldn't stop my father, you know." (1.5.268)

Thought: We can interpret the common thread here as Lady Marchmain, not as genetic predisposition to alcoholism.

"It's no good, Charles," she said. "All you can mean is that you have not as much influence or knowledge of him as I thought. It is no good either of us trying to believe him. I've known drunkards before. One of the most terrible things about them is their deceit. Love of truth is the first thing that goes." (1.5.375)

Thought: Lady Marchmain doesn't seem to have much knowledge of Sebastian herself. He was always much more interested in beauty and happiness than he was in truth.

"Dear boy," said Lady Marchmain. "How nice to see you looking so well again. Your day in the open has done you good. The drinks are on the table; do help yourself."

There was nothing unusual in her speech but the fact of her saying it. Six months ago it would not have been said.

"Thanks," said Sebastian. "I will." (1.6.188-90)

Thought: Lady Marchmain has given up on controlling Sebastian's drinking – but why? What pushed her over the edge this time?

Next morning I said to Sebastian: "Tell me honestly, do you want me to stay on here?"

"No, Charles, I don't believe I do."

"I'm no help?"

"No help." (1.6.202-5)

Thought: Charles is no help…with what? Sebastian's family? His alcoholism? Religion? Depression? What is he referring to here?

Society and Class Quotes

"He came to Le Touquet at Easter and, in some extraordinary way, I seemed to have asked him to stay. Well, my mother is used to me, but my poor stepfather found Mulcaster very hard to understand. You see my stepfather is a d-d-dago and therefore has a very high opinion of the English aristocracy. He couldn't quite fit Mulcaster into his idea of a lord, and really I couldn't explain him; he lost some infinitesimal sum at cards, and as a result expected me to pay for all his treats." (1.2.30)

Thought: Mulcaster proves that aristocratic blood does not a gentleman make.

"That, my dear, seemed to put a little life into them, and up the stairs they came, clattering. About six of them came into my room, the rest stood mouthing outside. My dear, they looked too extraordinary. They had been having one of their ridiculous club dinners, and they were all wearing coloured tail-coats – a sort of livery. 'My dears,' I said to them, 'you look like a lot of most disorderly footmen.'" (1.2.31)

Thought: *Brideshead Revisited* often makes fun of this sort of useless aristocratic tradition.

"I became very rich. It used to worry me, and I thought it wrong to have so many beautiful things when others had nothing. Now I realize that it is possible for the rich to sin by coveting the privileges of the poor. The poor have always been the favourites of God and His saints, but I believe that it is one of the special achievements of Grace to sanctify the whole of life, riches included. Wealth in pagan Rome was necessarily something cruel; it's not any more." (1.5.202)

Thought: Lady Marchmain struggles with her faith the same way that her children do. She may give the impression of perfect holiness, but Charles sees that she, too, doubts her ability to be a good Catholic. Even still, she uses her religion as a way to justify her own material wealth.

When I first met her, when she met me in the station yard and drove me home through the twilight that high summer of 1923, she was just eighteen and fresh from her first London season.

Some said it was the most brilliant season since the war, that things were getting into their stride again. Julia, by right, was at the centre of it. […] the ball given for Julia […] was by all accounts a splendid spectacle. Sebastian went down for it and half-heartedly suggested my coming with

him; I refused and came to regret my refusal, for it was the last ball of its kind given there; the last of a splendid series. (1.7.3-5)

Thought: Many critics have commented on *Brideshead*'s seeming nostalgia for aristocracy. Charles recognizes that the days of opulence and classism are coming to a close, and he fittingly places Julia right in the center of it. She is the symbol of beauty from a former time – not unlike the idea of her as a quattrocento beauty.

She outshone by far all the girls of her age, but she knew that, in that little world within a world which she inhabited, there were certain grave disabilities from which she suffered. [...] There was the scandal of her father; they had all loved him in the past, the women along the wall, and they most of them loved her mother, yet there was that slight, inherited stain upon her brightness that seemed deepened by something in her own way of life – waywardness and willfulness, a less disciplined habit than most of her contemporaries' – that unfitted her for the highest honours; but for that, who knows? (1.7.13)

Thought: Remember Charles and Cordelia's discussion of the word "thwarted"? This is what Julia is – all unfulfilled potential. Interestingly enough, Charles finds her all the more beautiful for this reason.

As it seemed to her, the thing was a dead loss. If she apostatized now, having been brought up in the Church, she would go to hell, while the Protestant girls of her acquaintance, schooled in happy ignorance, could marry eldest sons, live at peace with their world, and get to heaven before her. There could be no eldest son for her, and younger sons were indelicate things, necessary, but not to be much spoken of. [...] There were of course the Catholics themselves, but these came seldom into the little world Julia had made for herself; those who did were her mother's kinsmen, who, to her, seemed grim and eccentric. Of the dozen or so wealthy and noble Catholic families, none at that time had an heir of the right age. Foreigners – there were many among her mother's family – were tricky about money, odd in their ways, and a sure mark of failure in the English girl who wed them. What was there left? (1.7.16)

Thought: Religion and class concerns run Julia's life and restricts her choices, the same as it does for Sebastian.

Here I am, I thought, back from the jungle, back from the ruins. Here, where wealth is no longer gorgeous and power has no dignity. Quomodo sedet sola civitas (for I had heard that great lament, which Cordelia once quoted to me in the drawing-room of Marchmain House, sung by a half-caste choir in Guatemala, nearly a year ago). (2.1.101)

Thought: Charles has come back to England to discover the "charm" which Anthony claimed so devastated him and his art.

In token of her appreciation the chief purser had been asked to our party and he, in token of his appreciation, had sent before him the life-size effigy of a swan, moulded in ice and filled with caviar. This chilly piece of magnificence now dominated the room, standing on a table in the centre, thawing gently, dripping at the beak into its silver dish. The flowers of the morning delivery hid as much as possible of the panelling (for this room was a miniature of the monstrous hall above). (2.1.137)

Thought: Just like Rex's diamond-encrusted tortoise, the ice swan filled with caviar is the perfect picture of vulgar extravagance. To Charles, who has just returned from the jungles of South America, this must seem a particularly despicable display of wealth.

"'He is quite sane and quite in earnest. He wanted to go to the bush, as far away as he could get, among the simplest people, to the cannibals. The Superior said: 'We have no cannibals in our missions.' He said, well, pygmies would do, or just a primitive village somewhere on a river; or lepers – lepers would do best of anything.'" (2.4.75)

Thought: Sebastian's desires are similar to Charles's reasons for heading to South America: he wants to escape "British charm."

Love Quotes

Here my last love died. There was nothing remarkable in the manner of its death. One day, not long before this last day in camp, as I lay awake before reveille, [...] in that dark hour, I was aghast to realize that something within me, long sickening, had quietly died, and felt as a husband might feel, who, in the fourth year of his marriage, suddenly knew that he had no longer any desire, or tenderness, or esteem, for a once-beloved wife; [...] we had been through it together, the army and I, from the first importunate courtship until now, when nothing remained to us except the chill bonds of law and duty and custom. [...] She was stripped of all enchantment now and I knew her for an uncongenial stranger to whom I had bound myself indissolubly in a moment of folly. (prologue.5)

Thought: Charles once called Sebastian the "forerunner" to his love for Julia, and wondered if everyone he loved successively was just a forerunner to something else. It looks like the army came after Julia; does the end of the novel leave any hope for a new love for Charles?

I could tell him, too, that to know and love one other human being is the root of all wisdom. But I felt no need for these sophistries as I sat before my cousin [...]. So I told him what was not in fact the truth, that I usually had a glass of champagne about that time, and asked him to join me. (1.2.21)

Thought: I could tell him, too, that to know and love one other human being is the root of all wisdom. But I felt no need for these sophistries as I sat before my cousin [...]. So I told him what was not in fact the truth, that I usually had a glass of champagne about that time, and asked him to join me. (1.2.21)

She so much resembled Sebastian that, sitting beside her in the gathering dusk, I was confused by the double illusion of familiarity and strangeness. Thus, looking through strong lenses one may watch a man approaching from afar, study every detail of his face and clothes, believe one has only to put out a hand to touch him, marvel that he does not hear one, and look up as one moves, and then seeing him with the naked eye suddenly remember that one is to him a distant speck, doubtfully human. I knew her and she did not know me. (1.3.116)

Thought: Charles's love for Julia is only a misplaced desire for her brother Sebastian. He's only attracted to her for her physical resemblance to him.

"It is a kind of love that comes to children before they know its meaning. In England it comes when you are almost men; I think I like that. It is better to have that kind of love for another boy than for a girl. Alex you see had it for a girl, for his wife." (1.4.229)

Thought: Is Cara correct in comparing Lord Marchmain's love for his wife with Charles's love for Sebastian? Does Charles ever come to despise Sebastian the way Lord Marchmain does his wife? Or is he spared this emotion because Sebastian is another man?

She had made a preposterous little picture of the kind of man who would do [...] and she was in search of him when she met me at the railway station. I was not her man. She told me as much, without a word, when she took the cigarette from my lips. (1.7.18)

Thought: Julia isn't capable of loving Charles when she first meets him because she hasn't grown up yet. It's not until she realizes how silly her preconceptions about love and marriage are, and how absurd her prerequisites for a husband, that she becomes an adult.

All this I learned about Julia, bit by bit, from the stories she told, from guesswork, knowing her, from what her friends said, from the odd expressions she now and then let slip, from occasional dreamy monologues of reminiscences; I learned it as one does learn the former – as it seems at the time, the preparatory – life of a woman one loves, so that one thinks of oneself as part of it, directing it by devious ways, towards oneself. (1.7.19)

Thought: Notice how Charles hints at his eventual love affair with Julia before we are told of it explicitly.

From being agreeable, he became indispensable to her; from having been proud of him in public she became a little ashamed, but by that time, between Christmas and Easter, he had become indispensable. And then, without in the least expecting it, she suddenly found herself in love. (1.7.28)

Thought: Julia's love with Rex stems from convenience, whereas for love for Charles is one of deep emotional need.

"You didn't wonder if I should have fallen in love with someone else in the meantime?"

"No. Have you?"

"You know I haven't. Have you?"

"No. I'm not in love." (2.1.51-4)

Thought: Talk about a loaded conversation. Charles doesn't mean that he hasn't fallen in love with anyone else; he means that he isn't in love at all – even with his wife.

"I'm glad about the roses," said Julia. "Frankly, they were a shock. They made me think we were starting the day on quite the wrong footing."

I knew what she meant, and in that moment felt as though I had shaken off some of the dust and grit of ten dry years; then and always, however she spoke to me – in half sentences, single words, stock phrases of contemporary jargon, in scarcely perceptible movements of eyes or lips or hands – however inexpressible her thought, however quick and far it had glanced from the matter in hand, however deep it had plunged, as it often did, straight from the surface to the depths, I knew; even that day when I still stood on the extreme verge of love, I knew what she meant. (2.1.290-1)

Thought: Love in *Brideshead Revisited* is all about the ability to communicate. Charles and Sebastian shared this, and now he and Julia have the same bond.

Perhaps […] all our loves are merely hints and symbols; a hill of many invisible crests; doors that open as in a dream to reveal only a further stretch of carpet and another door; perhaps you and I are types and this sadness which sometimes falls between us springs from disappointment in our search, each straining through and beyond the other, snatching a glimpse now and then of the shadow which turns the corner always a pace or two ahead of us.

I had not forgotten Sebastian. He was with me daily in Julia; or rather it was Julia I had known in him, in those distant, Arcadian days. (2.4.67-8)

Thought: If what Charles says is true – if people like Sebastian and Julia are merely temporary vessels for some sort of lifelong emotion – does that undermine or devalue his relationships with them?

"You and Julia . . ."she said. And then, as we moved on towards the house, "When you met me last night did you think, 'Poor Cordelia, such an engaging child, grown up a plain and pious spinster, full of good works'? Did you think 'thwarted'?"

It was no time for prevarication. "Yes," I said, "I did; I don't now, so much."

"It's funny," she said, "that's exactly the word I thought of for you and Julia. When we were up in the nursery with Nanny. Thwarted passion,' I thought." (2.4.97-100)

Thought: Compare this to Anthony's description of Charles's paintings from South America – he seems to think that Charles's talent has been "thwarted," too. Looks like more of that connection between love and art.

Plot Analysis

Classic Plot Analysis

Initial Situation
Sebastian pukes into Charles's first floor window.
This is the start of a beautiful friendship. Sebastian's eccentricities captivate Charles's attention and draw him into the "enchanted garden" he so hoped to find at Oxford.

Conflict
Sebastian's family, religion, the danger of "charm"
Anthony Blanche's long lecture to Charles over dinner sets us up for all the novel's greatest conflicts. He calls Julia a "heathen," points out that Sebastian is essentially just an insipid bore, warns Charles of the entire Flyte family but particularly Lady Marchmain, and draws our attention to what he considers the greatest threat to Charles's artistry: charm.

Complication
Sebastian's alcoholism, Samgrass, Julia and Charles's love
Sebastian's attempt to solve the conflict (his family, his religion) by drinking only makes things worse. He grows more and more depressed as he sinks deeper into self-imposed isolation. On top of that, he and Charles both have to deal with Samgrass, a.k.a. The Most Annoying Family Friend Ever. And that's all before Charles falls in love with Julia – despite each of their marriages to another.

Climax
The Big Twitch Upon the Thread
After several months of anticipatory death-bed action, Lord Marchmain finally returns to Catholicism, moments before he dies. This is the event that spurs Charles's own later conversion.

Suspense

The Big Twitch Upon the Thread

Charles's foreshadowing metaphor of the ice fisher minutes away from a devastating avalanche is a good clue that something's up with Julia and his relationship. It's only a matter of time before the situation comes to a head. We're also wondering who is going to end up living at Brideshead, since Lord Marchmain has promised it to Charles and Julia, but we know but we know from the prologue that this isn't the end result.

Denouement

Julia breaks it off with Charles; Charles gets final updates on everyone's life from Nanny in the epilogue

You can definitely feel the novel winding down even as Julia ends her affair with Charles. (And not just because you notice you're twenty pages from the end, either.) When Charles hears the latest news from Nanny Hawkins, it's classic denouement territory, as information is revealed and any lingering questions answered.

Conclusion

Charles visits the chapel at Brideshead

Amazingly, Charles has found faith and become a Catholic in between the end of his narrative and the start of the epilogue. The novel's conclusion is surprisingly optimistic, and you can read all about it in "What's Up With the Ending?"

Booker's Seven Basic Plots Analysis: Voyage and Return

Anticipation Stage and 'Fall' into the Other World

Charles seeks a "low door in the wall" as an entrance to an "enchanted garden." Then he meets Sebastian.

The 'other world' here is a metaphorical one, and consists largely of Sebastian's appreciation for beauty. It all begins with the trip to the botanical gardens. Of course, Brideshead Castle plays a large role in constituting this 'other world' as well.

Initial Fascination or Dream Stage

Charles is captivated by Sebastian, his eccentricities, and the world he lives in, particularly Brideshead.

As a burgeoning artist, it makes sense that Charles would be so taken in by the splendor of Brideshead Castle. He spends pages describing its design, architecture, and furnishings.

Frustration Stage

Lady Marchmain's machinations, Sebastian's drinking, Samgrass's general existence

The perfect world starts to crumble when Charles realizes the extent to which religion and family torment Sebastian. He chooses to side with his friend, which means making a temporary enemy of Lady Marchmain. Samgrass frustrates matters further, especially since he imposes restrictions for the boys even at Oxford.

Nightmare Stage

Charles is carrying on an affair with Julia and may be cheating Bridey out of his rightful inheritance.
Charles has become a part of the world of Brideshead Castle, but it isn't all sunshine and rainbows. He senses a darker side to himself correlating to what he discovered as the darker element of this 'other world.'

Thrilling Escape and Return
After Julia breaks up with Charles, he converts to Catholicism and joins the army.
Charles 'escapes' the world of Brideshead and returns to reality, leaving the Flyte family behind him completely. The interpretation of this conclusion as an 'escape' is certainly subject to debate, since he was really more evicted than anything else. It's also subject to debate whether or not leaving was a positive thing for Charles, or an unhappy bit of tragedy.

Three Act Plot Analysis

Act I
Charles meets Sebastian and makes several trips to Brideshead, where he is captivated by the estate and drawn into the Flyte family and all the baggage that goes with them.

Act II
Sebastian becomes an alcoholic, Julia's marriage to Rex is on the rocks, Charles hates his wife, his paintings are easy and boring, and Lady Marchmain has died without reconciling with her son. The affair between Charles and Julia begins.

Act III
Charles and Julia eventually break up, Lord Marchmain dies, and Cordelia predicts Sebastian's death.

Study Questions

1. Take a look at the cover picture on your book or, if you're not using the American edition, then check out the image here. Now for our Super Important Question: which character is which? What makes you think so? What is this cover saying about the novel? And, most importantly, ARE THEY PLAYING FOOTSIE!?
2. Think about the way time is manipulated in *Brideshead Revisited*, particularly the way Charles reveals his marriage to Celia and his affair with Julia. We jump around a lot in time as the details become clear. What is the effect of this sort of narration?
3. Here's another plot structure question for you: why is Lord Marchmain's death the novel's finale? Isn't he a minor character? Who cares if he dies?
4. What shifts do you see – in theme, tone, style, plot structure, or anything else – between Book One and Book Two of *Brideshead Revisited*?
5. Besides Charles, whose side are you on as a reader, and which characters just aren't

likeable? What do you think of Lady Marchmain, for example? Julia? Brideshead? Lord Marchmain?

Characters

All Characters

Charles Ryder Character Analysis

Charles and Sebastian
Talk about an enigmatic relationship. These two meet when Sebastian pukes into Charles's bedroom window. Charles is vehemently warned against him and in fact the entire Flyte family. And Sebastian has got to be the oddest duck in the Oxford pond. So what draws our protagonist to him?

Charles was admittedly on the look-out for something or someone at the time he met Sebastian. In his first few weeks at school he "felt at heart that this was not all that Oxford had to offer." It seems he was harboring romantic illusions about a world of intellect, aesthetics, and youthful verve that he just couldn't find among the majority of his peers. Check this out:

I was in search of love in those days, and I went full of curiosity and the faint, unrecognized apprehension that here, at last, I should find that low door in the wall, which others, I knew, had found before me, which opened on an enclosed and enchanted garden, which was somewhere, not overlooked by any window, in the heart of that grey city.

It is Sebastian who leads Charles into this enchanted garden, inhabited by his slew of equally eccentric but contagiously enthusiastic friends.

Sebastian also provides two things Charles didn't have on his own: a childhood, and a full family. As Charles says: "That summer term with Sebastian, it seemed as though I was being given a brief spell of what I had never known, a happy childhood" (1.2.18). He also claims that he's "rather curious about people's families" as "it's not a thing [he] know[s] about" because there's "only [his] father and [him]self." Can you start to see the appeal for him in a person like Sebastian? (For oodles more on Sebastian's obsession with youth and of course his impossible family, read his own "Character Analysis.")

Of course, some would argue that Charles's attraction to Sebastian is just that – physical attraction. There's been plenty of speculation on the possibly gay relationship between these two. It's mostly based on Charles's comment that he and Sebastian took part in "naughtiness

high in the catalogue of grave sins." Sure, this could be talking about sodomy…but then again maybe not. Charles and Sebastian were constantly drunk and, as we know from the Old Hundredth incident, probably not strangers to brothels. The "naughtiness" Charles mentions could just as easily refer to either (or both) of these. The other commentary to consider is Cara's, later in the novel. Of Charles and Sebastian she says: "I know of these romantic friendships of the English and the Germans. They are not Latin. I think they are very good if they do not go on too long." The important thing to remember here is that "romantic" doesn't necessarily mean "sexual." The other thing to take into consideration is Anthony, who is definitely gay (see his "Character Analysis" for more) and the way Charles reacts to and judges him for it.

We think the take-home lesson is this: it doesn't really matter whether Charles and Sebastian are sexually involved. Either way, we know that they love each other fiercely, and the possibility of sexual relationship doesn't really change the significance of their relationship in the novel. It's not about sex. (And it's not about money either. Charles comes from wealth himself, so isn't a "poor kid meets rich guy" story.) Rather, their relationship is about beauty.

That's right – Sebastian is Charles's instructor in aesthetics. Notice that the first thing these two do alone is visit the Botanical Gardens – at Sebastian's suggestion, or course. Sebastian's comment is: "Oh, Charles, what a lot you have to learn!" as he leads the way. When he returns to his rooms, Charles has the first inkling of dislike for his wall decorations (which in retrospect he knows to be in poor taste). He turns away the screen of daffodils, his first step in shedding his immature ideas about what makes good art. Charles also explicitly credits Sebastian with this sort of aesthetic instruction when he says, "Collins had exposed the fallacy of modern aesthetics to me, […] but it was not until Sebastian, idly turning the pages of Clive Bell's *Art*, read '"Does anyone feel the same kind of emotion for a butterfly or a flower that he feels for a cathedral or a picture?" Yes, I do,' that my eyes were opened" (1.1.27). Sebastian himself possesses an "epicene beauty" and so fits well into the world to which he lures Charles. Brideshead Castle, of course, is at the center of this new world of art and beauty, and our narrator even deems it "an aesthetic education to live within those walls." You can see why Charles, a burgeoning artist, would be so attracted to a 'teacher' like Sebastian and the "glittering world," as Waugh calls it, in which he lives.

Once they are good friends, Charles defends Sebastian with unwavering loyalty. Their friendship seems to flourish only in self-imposed isolation from the rest of the world – *contra mundum*, as Charles says it. Sebastian certainly tests this loyalty again and again. Will Charles side with the Flytes against his friend? Will he be swayed by Lady Marchmain's pleas? Will he listen to Anthony's warnings about Sebastian? Will he help fight Sebastian's alcoholism? Charles answers "no" to all of these, placing Sebastian's happiness above all else, even his health. How is it, then, that their friendship crumbles by the second half of the novel? Sebastian's Character Analysis is up next, so stay tuned. Meanwhile, let's talk about Julia.

Charles, Julia, and Love
The big question regarding Charles and Julia is this: does he love her because she's the female equivalent of Sebastian? When Charles first meets Julia, what strikes him about her is

her uncanny resemblance to her brother; "She so much resemble[s] Sebastian that, sitting beside her in the gathering dusk, [he is] confused by the double illusion of familiarity and strangeness" (1.3.108). In fact, "her sex [is] the [only] palpable difference between the familiar and the strange." Shortly after, Sebastian comments that "she's so like [him]," but only "in looks" and in "the way she talks." But the big honking tip-off comes towards the end of the novel, when Charles for the second time refers to his friendship with Sebastian as "the forerunner" to his relationship with Julia. Then he says that "Sebastian is with [him] daily in Julia," which really makes you wonder whether he isn't just using her to recapture the one relationship which shaped his days as a younger man.

The answer to this question lies in the way that Charles understands love. When you read the novel with this question in mind, you start to see that *Brideshead Revisited* is the story not only of Charles's aesthetic education, but also his journey to define this difficult emotion. He comes to Oxford "in search of love" and thinks he finds it in Sebastian. Cara is his next instructor, explaining to him the nature of his love for Sebastian and the difference between a man's first love – the love boys have when they are "almost men" – and his second, mature love. We can assume that Julia is this second love of Charles, but things get complicated when she asks the difficult question: what if she is just a forerunner, too?

Now Charles devises a new theory for himself: "Perhaps all our loves are merely hints and symbols; a hill of many invisible crests; doors that open as in a dream to reveal only a further stretch of carpet and another door [...], the shadow which turns the corner always a pace or two ahead of us." Julia is correct to worry that Charles's love will find a new object after her, and we know from the prologue that it is in fact the army. Of course, Charles says in the novel's opening: "Here, love died between me and the army" and in its closing refers to himself as "loveless." Oops. First Sebastian, then Julia, then the army – is there any hope for another object of love for Charles? Is this what his journey has brought him to – a loveless middle-aged Captain in the army?

Before you get too depressed, jump all the way back to Charles's second conversation with Jasper, in Book One, Chapter Two, when Charles muses that "to know and love one other human being is the root of all wisdom." Wise words for a man just beginning his education in art and love, right? This is where we have to wonder WHO is responsible for this little platitude – Charles the twenty-something at Oxford, or Charles the middle-aged narrator? (Check out "Point of View" for a full discussion of this ever-present uncertainty in the novel.) It's very possible that this line is the culmination of everything Charles has learned about love over the course of his life. And how funny that it comes in at the *start* of his recollection.

Charles, Art, and God
Does anyone else think art is basically a religion for the agnostic Charles? Here are a few passages to consider:

I held back from painting, like a diver on the water's edge; once in I found myself buoyed and exhilarated. I was normally a slow and deliberate painter; that afternoon and all next day, and the day after, I worked fast. I could do nothing wrong. At the end of each passage I paused,

tense, afraid to start, the next, fearing, like a gambler, that luck must turn and the pile be lost. Bit by bit, minute by minute, the thing came into being. There were no difficulties; the intricate multiplicity of light and colour became a whole; the right colour was where I wanted it on the palette; each brush stroke, as soon as it was complete, seemed to have been there always.

Dos this sound like divine inspiration to you? Because Charles certainly thinks so:

I had felt the brush take life in my hand that afternoon; I had had my finger in the great, succulent pie of creation. I was a man of the Renaissance that evening – of Browning's Renaissance. I, who had walked the streets of Rome in Genoa velvet and had seen the stars through Galileo's tube, spurned the friars with their dusty tomes and their sunken, jealous eyes and their crabbed hair-splitting speech.

And later he adds: "I began to mourn the loss of something I had known in the drawing-room of Marchmain House and once or twice since, the intensity and singleness and the belief that it was not all done by hand – in a word, the inspiration" (2.1.7). Others recognize this connection, too, particularly Brideshead: "You take art as a means not an end. That is strict theology, but it's unusual to find an agnostic believing it" (1.4.154).

Indeed, aesthetics are Charles's theology. (He might have learned this from Sebastian, who believes in things because they are lovely.) As such, his whole life is devoted to art. Or, as Celia says, "Charles lives for one thing – Beauty." That's why he's a painter, and it's certainly one possible basis for his love for Julia, a "flawless Florentine Quattrocento beauty." Read Book Two, Chapter One again (when Charles begins his affair with Julia) and notice how obsessed he is with her looks and the recent "completion of her beauty." Celia claims that Charles went to South America because he "got bored" with finding beauty in England. Now that he's come back, he needs a new artistic pursuit– and Julia is his next aesthetic conquest.

If Charles has such a sound personal theology through his pursuit of art and beauty, how is it that he ends up a Catholic by the time he's a middle-aged Captain in the army? Go read "What's Up With the Ending?" and find out.

Charles Ryder Timeline and Summary

- Charles and his troops arrive at Brideshead Castle in the early 1940s. He begins his flashback.
- Charles and Sebastian take a short road trip to Brideshead together.
- Charles recalls listening to (and subsequently ignoring) Jasper's advice and first meeting Sebastian and his friends, like Anthony Blanche.
- We return to the road trip and Charles's first visit to Brideshead. He meets Nanny Hawkins and learns that Sebastian doesn't like his family.
- Jasper tells Charles that he's doing horribly, socially speaking.
- Anthony takes Charles out to dinner and tells him all about Sebastian's family. Charles disregards anything that negatively portrays Sebastian.

- Charles goes home for the summer; many uncomfortable dinners with his father follow.
- He gets news that Sebastian is dying and rushes off to Brideshead, only to hear from Julia that Sebastian's broken a small bone in his foot. (Note the way Charles perceives Julia, as a female version of Sebastian.)
- Charles spends the summer alone at Brideshead with Sebastian getting drunk on the estate's wine collection. They discuss religion: Sebastian struggles with Catholicism; Charles is an agnostic.
- Charles meets Cordelia and Bridey.
- He travels to Venice with Sebastian and meets Lord Marchmain and Cara. He is informed that Sebastian is an alcoholic.
- The second year at Oxford is decidedly less fun; Anthony has gone and Lady Marchmain keeps trying to keep her son in line (buzz kill!).
- Charles meets (and dislikes) Mr. Samgrass.
- Charles meets Rex Mottram and is invited to a charity ball. With Boy and Sebastian he sneaks away to Ma Mayfield's. After some heavy partying, they are arrested for drunk driving on the way home. They call Rex, who gets them out of jail for the night.
- Back at Oxford, Charles and Sebastian are gated for the term.
- At Brideshead over the Christmas vacation, Lady Marchmain tries to befriend Charles. This angers Sebastian.
- Charles takes Sebastian to his home in London, where Mr. Ryder finds him amusing.
- Back at Oxford, Charles notes that Sebastian's drinking and depression are worsening.
- At Easter at Brideshead, Sebastian makes a drunken fool out of himself in front of the family. Then he takes off without Charles.
- Charles is left alone with Lady Marchmain, who tells him all about the book she's putting together to commemorate her dead brother Ned.
- Charles looks over the book but decides that he is on Sebastian's side, against the rest of the world.
- Lady Marchmain visits Oxford and asks Charles if Sebastian is drinking too much again. He says no, but later that night Sebastian is found stumbling around drunk. Lady Marchmain expresses a wish for Sebastian to live with Monsignor Bell, since he isn't strong enough to keep his Catholic faith alone.
- Charles is miserable after Sebastian leaves Oxford. Next Christmas, he joins them all again at Brideshead. He is concerned for Sebastian's health.
- Charles discovers that Samgrass is lying about his time with Sebastian; in truth, Sebastian escaped and has been drinking.
- Charles gives Sebastian money to go to a bar with. When Lady Marchmain finds out, she guilts Charles about it. Charles asks Sebastian if he should stay at Brideshead. When he hears no, he leaves.
- Charles gets a letter from Cordelia explaining that she's been sneaking money to Sebastian for booze too. Samgrass was found out and left the estate as well, and Rex is taking Sebastian to a doctor in Germany to see about fixing that alcoholism.
- Rex comes to see Charles in Paris. He explains that Lady Marchmain feels bad about blaming Charles for Sebastian. He says he wants to marry Julia but that her mother is against it. He also admits to having an affair with Brenda Champion.
- In his narration, Charles discourses on Julia for a bit and explores his perceptions of her character and her reasons for marrying Rex. We get the story of their relationship, engagement, and ultimate marriage.

- In 1926 Charles returns to London and bumps into Anthony and Boy. Anthony tells him about Sebastian's condition and his new friend Kurt.
- Julia runs into Charles. She tells him that her mother is dying and wants to see him. Charles goes to see Lady Marchmain, who asks him to get Sebastian for her.
- Charles travels to Morocco in search of Sebastian. He finds Kurt and talks to Sebastian, who is ill in a hospital bed.
- Charles returns to Brideshead after Lady Marchmain's death and meets up with Cordelia. They discuss religion over dinner.
- Charles becomes an architectural painter. He travels to South America for work.
- Charles meets up with his wife in America to take the ship back to Europe. We find out that his wife is Celia, Boy's sister, and that their marriage isn't going so well. Charles has two kids, one of whom he hasn't seen yet.
- Julia is aboard the ship as well. During a violent storm he and she begin an affair. He listens to Julia discuss her unhappy marriage to Rex.
- At the day of his exhibition, Charles meets Anthony Blanche. He tells him that his paintings aren't as virile and wild as the critics believe.
- Charles goes to Brideshead with Julia. He hears about Beryl.
- When Brideshead insults his sister, Charles has a hard time calming her down.
- Charles and Julia fight about religion; she hits him twice and then apologizes.
- Charles and Julia set about finalizing their divorces.
- Charles sees Cordelia again and thinks that her potential has been squandered. They chat with Nanny.
- Julia and Charles discuss Sebastian. Charles calls him to forerunner, which makes Julia nervous that she is the forerunner to someone else.
- Cordelia updates Charles on Sebastian. He is in Tunis, living at a monastery.
- When Lord Marchmain returns to Brideshead to die, Charles spends a good deal of time with him and Julia. He is thrilled though ashamed to admit it when Lord Marchmain announces that he wants to leave Brideshead to Charles and Julia, rather than to Bridey and Beryl.
- Charles, Julia, Brideshead, and Cordelia fight over whether or not Lord Marchmain should see a priest on his death bed. The religious wing wins out, and Charles finds himself hoping that the old man will show a sign that he believes in God.
- Julia breaks up with Charles.
- In the epilogue, we return to the middle-aged Charles telling his story. He explores the Brideshead estate and visits with Nanny Hawkins, who updates him on the family.
- Before he leaves, Charles finds himself driven by the flame in the chapel to reflect optimistically on "the builders and the tragedians."

Lord Sebastian Flyte Character Analysis

Poor Sebastian. He goes from a beautiful, youthful, happy, and oblivious lad of nineteen to a depressed, alcoholic, self-loathing would-be caretaker of dying lepers. What happened? Let's start at the beginning, with three big aspects of Sebastian's very quirky character.

Sebastian and Youth

Cara says it best: "Sebastian is in love with his own childhood." He carries around a teddy-bear named Aloysius (named after Saint Aloysius, the patron of *youth*, by the way). The only positive relationship in his life – besides Charles – is with his Nanny, who for some reason still lives at Brideshead. Sebastian, like a child, is incessantly concerned with possession, even of people – Samgrass is "someone of Mummy's"; Rex is "someone of Julia's", etc. He gets so territorial about Charles because he applies these same childish rules of possession to their friendship. In his mind, Charles belongs to him, and his family can't intrude. (More on this in a bit.) And even Charles remarks that Sebastian provides him with the childhood he never had. Where did this all come from?

As a very wise group of Oompa Loompas once said, it's all the fault of the parents. Sebastian's family – or at least his mother – has babied him to death. Sebastian isn't even allowed the responsibility of his own allowance; "Mummy likes everything to be a present," he says. His relationship with Kurt is his shoddy attempt at finally taking care of someone else for once (more on that in Kurt's "Character Analysis"), which means he's starved for adult responsibility. For better or (more likely) for worse, Sebastian is stuck with youth. In fact, that's probably why we never see him grow old; he does so offstage, so to speak. In this novel, in Charles's recollection, Sebastian literally isn't allowed to grow up.

Sebastian and Aesthetics

We talked a lot about the role art plays in Charles's life and in his friendship with Sebastian in Charles's "Character Analysis." We claim that Sebastian is Charles's aesthetic instructor, and the more we look at Sebastian's character, the more we're convinced that…we're right. Right from the get-go Sebastian surrounds himself with beautiful things. He fills Charles's room with flowers as way of an apology. He takes him to the Botanical Gardens the first time they hang out together. The first scene Charles remembers at the very beginning of the novel is a picnic of wine and strawberries he shares outdoors with Sebastian. He even believes in Catholicism because the stories are lovely. And of course Sebastian himself is "magically beautiful, with that epicene quality that sings aloud for love and withers at the first cold wind." His wealth doesn't hurt either; it ensures that he is always steeped in opulent luxury, from the plover's eggs of his first lunch with Charles (a rare delicacy) to the expensive, fancy-shmancy Whatman H.P. Drawing paper he uses to scribble a quick note (in crayon!) in Charles's rooms. Sebastian exists in a world of wine, art, architectural splendor, and "the languor of youth," as Charles calls it.

Sebastian's Eccentricities

You know, besides the teddy bear. Sebastian has his own way of talking, acting, moving, and relating to others. For one, he is always working in imperatives and exaggerations, as Charles notices: "I *must* have pillar-box red pajamas," "I *have* to stay in bed until the sun works round to the windows," "I've absolutely *got* to drink champagne tonight," etc. (Even the *subject matter* of

these imperatives is luxurious and impulsive.) When he breaks a tiny bone in his foot, he writes Charles to say he's dying. He surrounds himself with characters as colorful as he (think Anthony Blanche). Charles notes that Sebastian writes letters "in a style of remote fantasy," but more importantly, this is how Sebastian *lives*.

Somehow, through all his peculiarities, Sebastian manages to charm everyone he meets. As Cordelia comments late in the novel of the monks in Tunisia, "They loved him there. He's still loved, you see, wherever he goes, whatever condition he's in. It's a thing about him he'll never lose." Charles realizes the same thing when he visits Sebastian in Morocco and finds that he's completely duped the "poor monk, poor booby" who believes the young man is all good intentions. The fact is, Sebastian is incredibly magnetic – or "charming," as Anthony calls him. (In fact, Anthony is the only one to see through the charm and pronounce Sebastian simply "insipid" if not completely boring. This has to do with Anthony's insight on "charm" and its dangers – but we'll talk about that in Anthony's "Character Analysis.") This magnetism means that those who love Sebastian – who truly love him – do so unconditionally. Think in particular about Cordelia and Charles. They love the whole package: the alcoholism, the insipidness, the immaturity, the selfishness. As Charles notes, "there [is] no past tense in Cordelia's verb 'to love.'" Despite the mess he's gotten himself into, she still loves her brother wholeheartedly. And so does Charles – notice that these two are the only characters to sneak him booze during the family's attempt at an intervention. They simply love him too much to see him suffer. This is, however, more than we can say for the rest of Sebastian's family. (See "Tools of Characterization"; the way Sebastian's various siblings react to his alcoholism – carelessness or mild annoyance – is proof enough.)

Religion, Family, Alcohol and Depression

Sadly, the three character points we just covered – obsession with youth, preoccupation with beauty, and an eccentric magnetism – all set Sebastian up to fall, hard. And fall he does. Love of youth is an obvious one, since this is no Never Never Land. (Or, as our favorite analysis chick Cara says, "Sebastian is in love with his own youth. That will make him very unhappy.") Sebastian's world of aesthetics is an extremely delicate one, threatening to shatter at any point, as evidenced by Charles's description of his beauty: "…with that epicene quality which […] withers at the first cold wind." ("Withers at the first cold wind" is the important part of this sentence.) And Sebastian's eccentric personality, while it is magnetic, means that he demands a very special sort of loyalty from those around him – a devotion that, as we've just seen, many can not give. So Sebastian spends the first quarter of the novel poised delicately at the cliff of depression, and the next three-quarters careening wildly down into it.

Of course Sebastian doesn't just fall – he's pushed by two majorly antagonistic forces: his family and his family's religion. These have been a problem from the start. Notice that Sebastian refers to Brideshead as the place "where [his] family live," NOT as his home. He even refers to his family in the same passage as "ravening beasts." He goes to great lengths to keep Charles away from them, for what turns out to be fairly good reason – they want to have him for themselves. "I'm not going to have you get mixed up with my family," he tells Charles. "All my life they've been taking things away from me. If they once got hold of you […] they'd make you their friend, not mine, and I won't let them."

As it turns out, Sebastian's suspicions are very much warranted. Lady Marchmain indeed does try to get Charles to help her control her son, and Charles inevitably feels guilty at any part he plays in her game. He recalls Sebastian weeping and asking, "Why do you take their side against me? I knew you would if I let you meet them. Why do you spy on me?" Charles adds in his narration that Sebastian "said more than [he] can bear to remember, even at twenty years' distance." Though he does agree to side with Sebastian against the world, Charles still recognizes that "as [his] intimacy with [Sebastian's] family [grows], [he] [becomes] part of the world which [Sebastian] sought to escape; [...] one of the bonds which held him."

So that covers family. What about religion? This, too, gets in the way of Charles and Sebastian's friendship. Notice that it is only after a series of conversations about religion that Charles says, "I began to realize how little I really knew of Sebastian, and to understand why he had always sought to keep me apart from the rest of his life. He was like a friend made on board ship, on the high seas; now we had come to his home port" (1.4.156). Charles doesn't understand religion – at all – which means there is a fundamental part of Sebastian's character that he can never access.

And it is exactly this part of Sebastian that drives him over the edge. Sebastian is tortured by the conflict between his *desire* to be happy and his *need* to be holy (a.k.a. to suffer). As Cordelia later says, he fits neither into the secular nor monastic world. At first, Sebastian isn't all together aware of this predicament. "Julia and I are half-heathen," he says. "I am happy, I rather think Julia isn't; [...] Anyway, however you look at it, happiness doesn't seem to have much to do with it, and that's all I want." Au contraire, Sebastian. Or as Charles later says, "Without [...] religion, Sebastian would have the chance to be a happy and healthy man" (1.4.85). Sebastian gradually comes to understand this conflict, stating that "it's very difficult being a Catholic" and praying, "Oh God, make me good, but not yet." As Sebastian's obligation to be holy overcomes his desire to be happy, he alienates himself from others ("count[ing] among the intruders his own conscience and all claims of human affection") and heads for a leper colony in Northern Africa.

What? A *leper* colony? At this point, the novel turns to Cordelia for a little explanation. (*Brideshead Revisited* has a habit of getting important information across through these minor female characters.) Cordelia narrates what's been happening with Sebastian in the last few years and describes his current situation in Tunis. There are any number of reasons Sebastian has gone to Northern Africa to live out the rest of his days. It could be that he still desperately wants to take care of someone or something, like he did with Kurt. This would explain his desire to live with lepers or "some small church by a river," since he "always wanted a river [...] which he could look after when the priest was away." It could be that he's desperately trying to abandon British aristocracy and the strain that wealth places on holiness (Lady Marchmain discusses this with Charles in Book One). Or, very possibly, Sebastian is living up to the words he spoke in Book One: "I couldn't care less, and I shall go on running away, as far and as fast as I can." (After all, Cordelia refers to his travels as "escaping to the savages," "escape" being the important word here…)

Most importantly, Cordelia makes it clear to Charles just how very holy Sebastian really is. "I've seen others like him," she says, "and I believe they are very near and dear to God." She then

proceeds to describe Sebastian's death for us. We never see what happens to Sebastian, and even when Charles gets last-minute, concluding updates about the other characters from Nanny Hawkins in the epilogue, Sebastian is never mentioned. This is the last we hear of him. Cordelia envisions her brother as "a great favorite with the old fathers," "disappear[ing] for two or three days every month or so" and then returning "disheveled and shamefaced and [...] more devout for a day or two and of course still "completely charming." "One morning," she predicts, "he'll be picked up at the gate dying." This passage feels like a conclusion, doesn't it? So while Sebastian doesn't actually die in the course of the novel, as readers we're content left with the image of Sebastian as this holy, tortured, dying soul or, as Charles earlier said, a harmless and isolated man "cough[ing] his heart out among the rum bottles."

Lord Sebastian Flyte Timeline and Summary

- Sebastian and Charles borrow Hardcastle's car to travel to Brideshead. They stop to eat lunch outside, and Sebastian comments that he wishes he could bury a pot of gold everywhere he's ever been happy, so he could come back and dig it up later when he's "old and miserable."
- We're introduced to Sebastian's teddy-bear, Aloysius.
- Flashback to Sebastian puking into Charles's first floor rooms and then having him over for lunch to repent.
- Sebastian introduces Charles to all his friends, including Anthony Blanche.
- Cut back to the first visit to Brideshead. Sebastian introduces Charles to Nanny Hawkins. He insists that they leave before Julia returns, and they in fact pass her on the road as they've leaving.
- Sebastian reveals that he doesn't like his family.
- Over Easter vacation, Sebastian sends letters "written in remote fantasy" to Charles.
- When Charles tries to confirm Anthony's description of Sebastian and his family, Sebastian denies it and discusses his bear, as Anthony predicted he would.
- Sebastian sends a letter to Charles that he is gravely ill. It turns out that he tripped over a croquet hoop and broken a tiny bone in his foot.
- Sebastian and Charles spend all summer at Brideshead together drinking old wine. They also paint the interior of the office room together.
- Sebastian has Charles draw the fountain at Brideshead and give it to Nanny Hawkins.
- Sebastian debates religion with Charles. Sebastian's beliefs are based on aesthetics.
- Sebastian introduces Charles to his sister, Cordelia.
- He takes Charles to Venice to visit his father and his mistress Cara.
- The next year at Oxford, Sebastian gets several talking-tos from Monsignor Bell and Mr. Samgrass, both friends of his mothers.
- Sebastian retreats into solitude, booze, and disliking Mr. Samgrass.
- Sebastian, Charles, and Boy accept Rex's invitation to go to the ball. Then the three men sneak out to party at Ma Mayfield's. They are arrested for drunk driving. Mr. Samgrass testifies on Sebastian's behalf, but the incident is all over the newspapers.
- Back at Oxford, both Sebastian and Charles are gated.
- Sebastian resents his mother's attempts to befriend Charles over the course of the

Christmas vacation.

- Sebastian asks Charles to take him away; they go to London together to stay with Charles's father.
- Back at Oxford, Sebastian continues to drink uncontrollably.
- At Brideshead for over Easter, Sebastian makes a spectacle of himself and leaves Charles at the estate alone with his family.
- When Charles finds Sebastian again in London, Sebastian asks if he's taken Lady Marchmain's side. Charles responds that he is with Sebastian, against the world.
- They return to Oxford and Sebastian is more depressed than ever. His mother wants him to live with Monsignor Bell for the year, and ultimately takes him away from Oxford.
- Sebastian stays with his father in Venice for a bit. He then travels through Europe with Mr. Samgrass as a chaperone.
- Next Christmas Sebastian returns to Brideshead. It soon becomes clear that he gave Mr. Samgrass the slip and went on an extended drinking binge.
- Lady Marchmain instructs the servants not to give Sebastian alcohol. He manages to sneak some anyway. He convinces Charles to give him money and during a family hunt runs off to a hotel bar.
- After Charles leaves Brideshead, Sebastian gets his little sister Cordelia to slip him booze. In desperation his mother sends him off to Zurich with Rex to try and fix that whole alcoholism thing.
- Through Anthony, we find out that Sebastian went to stay with him in France. He drank all day long and stole to finance his alcoholism. He's now taken up with a German sergeant in French Morocco.
- Charles finds Sebastian ill in Morocco. He seems unconcerned that his mother is dying and is too sick to travel to say good-bye anyway. He tells Charles that he enjoys taking care of Kurt, since his whole life people have been taking care of him.
- Sebastian reports on Sebastian. Kurt is dead and Sebastian had traveled to Tunis and begged himself into a monastery there. She predicts that he will spend the rest of his life trying to be holy and occasionally lapsing into bouts of drinking. She doesn't think this is too bad of a deal for her brother.

Lady Julia Flyte Character Analysis

First and foremost, Julia is beautiful. Everyone defines her this way, from Anthony's mention of her "flawless Florentine Quattrocento beauty" to Charles's succinct "unhurried, exquisite, unrepentant" description of her late arrival to a ball. In fact, we make an argument in Charles's "Character Analysis" that Julia's looks are the sole reason he falls in love with her. To start with, she so much resembles Sebastian (quite the beauty himself) that you wonder how much of Charles's attraction is misplaced desire for her brother.

Transference aside, he's clearly struck by her beauty more than anything else. When he meets her after several years apart aboard the ship on the Atlantic, this is his focus. "She [...] was approaching the zenith of her loveliness," he says. Even months after their affair begins, it is still her beauty that holds him captive. It's not just Charles, either – even Julia's own father values

her so highly because of her looks. When debating the details of his will, Lord Marchmain wonders aloud to whom he will leave Brideshead Castle. "I have rather a fancy the idea of for installing Julia here," he says. "So beautiful this evening, my dear; so beautiful always; much, much more suitable." He essentially decides to leave Brideshead to her solely on the basis of aesthetics.

But even if the men in her life don't notice, Julia is definitely more than a pretty face. For one, she's not your typical girl. Charles remarks that women are "a point of interest" to Julia, suggesting that she's an outsider to her own gender. She's got her fair share of stereotypically masculine personality traits: aboard the ship in the Atlantic she's the only women around not in bed sick from the storm. And when she finds out that her brother, Charles, and Boy went to a club of ill-repute together, her only response is: "I do think you might have taken me with you. The ball was positively lethal, and I've always longed to go to the Old Hundredth." Probably not the response they were expecting from a woman.

Unfortunately for Julia, it's not the 21st century. It's not even 1998. We're talking about the 1920s and '30s here, which means she has one job in life and one job only: get married. While Julia accepts this role without dispute in the early part of her life, by the time she's in a loveless marriage and aboard the ship with Charles, she's wondering if maybe there isn't more to life than being beautiful and quiet. Or, as Charles imagines her saying, "Surely I was made for some other purpose than this?" Or even, "I am beautiful. I am made for delight. But what do I get out of it? Where is my reward?"

Interestingly enough, Charles finds this malaise, this "haunting, magical sadness" to be "the completion of her beauty." Yet when the two of them begin their affair aboard the ship, he senses that she loses this sadness, that it is "replaced by an incommunicable content and tranquility." Julia finds someone who fulfills her – Charles – and so she stops asking if life has more to offer; she's already found the love she's looking for. So of course we have to worry when, later on at Brideshead and after she has wondered if their love will last, Charles looks at Julia and finds that "she ha[s] regained what [he] thought she had lost forever, the magical sadness which had drawn [him] to her, the thwarted look." Notice that this is when Charles envisions the ice fisher about to be destroyed by an avalanche. He can tell that Julia has already decided to break it off and is once again wondering what life holds for her.

Before you start feeling too bad for Julia, let's talk about her less attractive characteristics. We'll start with the negative review from Anthony (although, to be fair, pretty much everyone gets a negative review from Anthony): "She's […] smart. […] Nothing greenery-yallery about her. So gay, so correct, so unaffected. Dogs and children love her, other girls love her – my dear, she's a fiend – a passionless, acquisitive, intriguing, ruthless filler. I wonder if she's incestuous. I doubt it; all she wants is power. There ought to be an Inquisition especially set up to burn her" (1.2.42).

How accurate *is* this assessment of Julia Flyte? We're not sure, because we only see her through Charles's eyes. It seems the worst we can say about her is that she doesn't love her brother. She treats his alcoholism and depression with mild annoyance, calling him "boring" and making no attempts to aid him or even pretend to be concerned for his welfare. "*You* must deal with him," she tells Charles. "It's no business of mine."

It's odd that Julia is so unresponsive to her brother's plight, since she actually suffers the same quandary herself: the desire to be happy vs. the need to be holy. The difference is, while Sebastian seems to have a true calling to a life of holy suffering, it seems that Julia does not. She chooses God out of guilt and fear rather than love. But let's take a look.

First we've got Julia's guilt over "living in sin with Charles" as Brideshead calls it, while she is still married to Brideshead. She rants about the word "sin" for at least two pages, but here's a choice excerpt:

"Living in sin, with sin, by sin, for sin, every hour, every day, year in, year out. Waking up with sin in the morning, seeing the curtains drawn on sin, bathing it, dressing it, clipping diamonds to it, feeding it, showing it round, giving it a good time, putting it to sleep at night with a tablet of Dial if it's fretful. Always the same, like an idiot child carefully nursed, guarded from the world. 'Poor Julia,' they say, 'she can't go out. She's got to take care of her little sin. A pity it ever lived,' they say, 'but it's so strong. Children like that always are. Julia's so good to her little, mad sin.'"

Is it just us, or is Julia more worried about reputation than God? Now remember that Julia ditched her religion a long time ago, all the way back when she acted as Rex's mistress before they were married in order to keep him from seeing Brenda Champion. She's been suppressing her Catholic guilt for a decade or so by the time she decides to break it off with Charles. And her reasons for doing so?

"I saw to-day there was one thing unforgivable […]; to set up a rival good to God's. […] it may be a private bargain between me and God, that if I give up this one thing I want so much, however bad I am, He won't quite despair of me in the end."

This is important: *it's NOT that Julia is afraid of living in sin with Charles – it's that she's afraid of being happy.* As Cordelia said earlier, "No one is every holy without suffering," and that seems to be a key point reiterated time and time again in *Brideshead Revisited*. It seems that her decision seems to stem from fear – probably of damnation – rather than of love for God. Of course, this is only one perspective, and it gets back to the old "Is *Brideshead* pro or anti Catholic?" question that we addressed in the "Overview." According to Waugh, each character experiences the grace of God in a different way. That would mean that Julia's reformation here is genuine, that she (and Charles, and Sebastian, and Lord Marchmain) genuinely accept God's love and chooses a life of Catholicism. From this perspective, Julia isn't breaking up with Charles out of fear or guilt; she genuinely wants to be holy and suffer.

Lady Julia Flyte Timeline and Summary

- Charles passes Julia on her way to Brideshead as he and Sebastian are leaving from his first visit to the estate.
- Anthony describes Julia as intelligent, beautiful, and a fiend.

- Charles officially meets Julia when he's hurrying to Brideshead under the impression that Sebastian is dying. She informs him that Sebastian merely broke a small bone in his foot. Charles is captivated by her similarities to her brother.
- Julia comes to visit Charles and Sebastian at Oxford, bringing Rex Mottram with her. She and Rex invite the boys to a party.
- In the aftermath of the Ma Mayfield fiasco, Julia says she was bored at the ball and the men should have taken her with them – after all, she's always wanted to see Ma Mayfield's.
- When Charles tries to broach the topic of Sebastian's alcoholism with her, Julia is flippant and uncaring, calling her brother "boring."
- Julia is with the others at Brideshead over the Christmas holiday, just after Sebastian has returned from Europe with Mr. Samgrass and Lady Marchmain is trying to stop his drinking. Again she responds to her brother's alcoholism with casual annoyance. Charles concludes that she cares more about the family's reputation than his health or happiness.
- Julia receives a tortoise from Rex with her initials placed in the shell in diamonds.
- Rex later reports that Julia realized Samgrass was lying about Sebastian and called him on it in front of her mother.
- After Rex discusses his wishes to marry Julia, Charles explores her character. He claims he is so interested in her because she is so like Sebastian. When he first met her, she was 18 and trying to decide whom to marry. Rex's darker side appealed to her.
- Charles then recounts the way she and Rex met. He was having an affair with Brenda Champion and Julia was staying nearby with her Aunt. After they met, Rex pursued her relentlessly.
- One night, after flaking on hanging out with Julia, Rex spends the night with Brenda. Julia finds out. When Rex comes to make amends, they end up engaged. Julia explains that the only way she could justify her anger at Rex for sleeping with Brenda is by being involved with him herself.
- Julia and Rex start hooking up until Julia has a moral and religious crisis and cuts him off. So Rex gets it from Brenda Champion instead. Julia goes to her priest to explain why she needs to hook up with Rex premaritally, but he won't give her permission to do so. So she says screw it and starts up the monkey business with Rex again.
- When Rex can't get permission to marry Julia from Lady Marchmain, he gets it instead from Lord Marchmain.
- Julia gets him to convert to Catholicism, and then has to explain to him that, because he's already been married, they can't tie the knot in a Catholic ceremony. So they have it done in a Protestant church instead.
- Years later, Julia explains to Charles her reasons for marrying Rex: she was already deeply involved with him and wanted to make an honest woman of herself. She adds that Rex isn't a complete human being.
- Julia hears that Charles is in England again and contacts him, reporting that Lady Marchmain is dying. She asks Charles to fetch Sebastian back to say good-bye to his mother.
- Aboard his ship back to England from America, Charles and his wife Celia hang out with Julia. While Celia is bed-ridden with seasickness, Charles and Julia catch up.
- Charles believes that Julia's beauty is more complete than ever, in large part due to the store of sadness she possesses.
- Julia fills Charles in on her life. She and Rex tried to have a child, but it was born dead.

Rex didn't care because it was a girl. Julia reiterates that Rex is not a whole person, and adds that he doesn't really love her (nor she him).
- The two of them share an obvious ability to communicate beyond words with each other.
- Julia explains that she's lost her religion.
- The two of them begin their affair. Before parting ways, they make plans to meet in London.
- Julia continues her affair with Charles. Ultimately, they decide to both get divorces and marry each other.
- Charles joins Julia at Brideshead.
- When her brother Brideshead arrives, Julia learns of his engagement to Beryl. Bridey insults her and her now loose morals, as she's "living in sin" with Charles while still married to Rex.
- Julia, upset, makes her way outside to the fountain. She confesses to Charles that she believes what Rex said to be true.
- Later, while they argue about religion, Julia gets suddenly angry at Charles for his attitude and hits him twice before crying and apologizing.
- Julia spends time with her sister Cordelia when she comes to visit Brideshead Castle.
- Julia has a talk with Charles about his having forgotten Sebastian. She doesn't like him deeming Sebastian the "forerunner," as she worries she herself is just a forerunner to another love.
- Staring at Julia one night, Charles decides that she has regained what first drew him to her that night on the ship, the "store of magical sadness" that seems to say, "Surely I was made for some other purpose than this?"
- Julia stays at Brideshead with Charles, Bridey, and Cordelia while Lord Marchmain lives out his last months there. Her father explains that he plans to leave the estate to her and Charles, on account of his disdain for Beryl. Julia doesn't have a problem with this and doesn't think Brideshead will either.
- Julia fights with Charles regarding her father's Last Rites. She thinks he should have a priest at his death bed. Julia wins out, and Lord Marchmain even gives the sign of the cross before he dies.
- Afterwards, Julia breaks up with Charles. She explains that, in order for God to forgive her, she has to make a sacrifice – and she chooses to sacrifice the happiness she could have had with Charles.
- In the epilogue, the lieutenant-colonel reports that the estate still belongs to Julia.
- When Charles visits Nanny Hawkins, she reports that Julia is with Cordelia abroad, helping with the war efforts.

Lady Marchmain Character Analysis

Lady Marchmain seems perfectly nice, doesn't she? She's pious, refined, concerned for her children's well-being, and dealing quite wonderfully with the fact that her husband left her for another woman. So explain these reactions to her:

Anthony: *"She [...] keeps a small gang of enslaved and emaciated prisoners for her exclusive*

enjoyment. *She sucks their blood. You can see the tooth-marks all over Adrian Porson's shoulders when he is bathing. [...] He's bled dry; there's nothing left of him. There are five or six others of all ages and sexes, like wraiths following her round. They never escape once she's had her teeth into them. It is witchcraft. There's no other explanation."*

Sebastian: *"She really was a femme fatale, wasn't she. She killed at a touch."*

Anthony, again: *"What a poor time that woman is having! It only shows there's some justice in life."*

Is any of this true? Are any of these rather extreme descriptions justified? We can answer only through Charles's eyes, but let's take a look anyway. As he spends more and more time with Lady Marchmain, Charles does indeed confirm her manipulative nature. "One was never summoned for a little talk," he says of her, "or consciously led to it; it merely happened, when she wished to speak intimately, that one found oneself alone with her." Even her requests for help in handling Sebastian are laced with this apparently super-human ability to manipulate: "she took hold of her subject in a feminine, flirtatious way, circling, approaching, retreating, feinting; she hovered over it like a butterfly; she played 'grandmother's steps' with it, getting nearer the real point imperceptibly while one's back was turned, standing rooted when she was observed" (1.5.291).

Still, Charles doesn't write her off and officially side with Sebastian until he reads her little book on Uncle Ned. What's up with that book, anyway? Lady Marchmain says of her dead brothers, "They were three splendid men; Ned was the best of them. He was the last to be killed, and when the telegram came, as I knew it would come, I thought: 'Now it's my son's turn to do what Ned can never do now.' I was alone then. He was just going to Eton. If you read Ned's book you'll understand." It's not exactly clear from the text, but Lady Marchmain is trying to get Sebastian to take over the male responsibilities of her own family, since Ned (her last living brother) has now kicked the bucket. This isn't at all a happy arrangement for the carefree and youthful Sebastian, who wants only to be happy. Charles finally understands her intentions after reading the book on the train, which explains this little exchange:

"Did you have a 'little talk' with Mummy?"
"Yes."
"Have you gone over to her side?"
The day before I would have said: "There aren't two sides"; that day I said, "No, I'm with you, Sebastian contra mundum."

OK, OK, so the woman is manipulative. But does that really explain all the hostility we see? No, not completely. Fortunately, Cordelia comes to our analytical rescue one again. (Boy, is she handy or what?): "When people wanted to hate God they hated mummy." This makes particular sense for Lady Marchmain's children, who had Catholicism imposed upon them by their mother (and certainly not their father, who converted himself just to keep her happy). Since holiness means suffering, and Lady Marchmain is responsible for her children's obligation to holiness, it follows that she is responsible for their suffering. We can start to see why Sebastian or even Julia so resent her. As for Lord Marchmain, that's an entirely different story – and a different "Character Analysis."

Lady Marchmain Timeline and Summary

- Anthony provides Charles with the back-story on Lady Marchmain. She is a strict Catholic and Lord Marchmain converted in order to marry her. When he wanted a divorce, she refused on account of her religion. They are now separated and he lives in Venice with his mistress. He left his wife with everything – both Brideshead and Marchmain House and all the servants who went with them.
- Lady Marchmain keeps an eye on her son through her acquaintances at Oxford, particularly Monsignor Bell.
- While visiting Lord Marchmain in Venice, Charles gets more info from Cara. She says that Lord Marchmain's first love was Lady Marchmain, but that now he hates her and everyone who knows her.
- Lady Marchmain visits Sebastian and Charles at Oxford. She begins to try and befriend Charles.
- We find out that Lady Marchmain is creating a memorial book for her brother Ned, who died in World War I. In doing so she engages the help of Mr. Samgrass, a history don.
- After the drunk driving fiasco, Lady Marchmain is surprisingly calm with her son. Still, Sebastian is miserable at having to deal with her, though Charles doesn't understand why.
- Over the Christmas vacation at Brideshead, Lady Marchmain continues her efforts in trying to befriend Charles. She also tries to convert him to Catholicism, which doesn't help.
- From his conversations with her, Charles learns that Lady Marchmain married into money. She used to worry that being rich would get in the way of her religion.
- At Easter, Lady Marchmain is not pleased to hear Cordelia report on her son's drunkenness as the reason for his absence from dinner.
- After Sebastian leaves for London, Lady Marchmain takes Charles aside. She is concerned about her son's depression, and explains that Lord Marchmain used to drink this same way – both men were ashamed of being unhappy.
- She asks for Charles's help in managing Sebastian, and also gives him a copy of the book she's putting together re: Ned for him to read. Charles realizes she's trying to manipulate him when he reads the book over.
- Lady Marchmain visits Oxford and asks Charles if Sebastian has been drinking. Charles tells her no, but Sebastian is found drunk that very night. Lady Marchmain takes him away from Oxford.
- The following Christmas, Lady Marchmain has instructed the servants not to give Sebastian any alcohol. When she finds out that Charles has been sneaking him booze, she guilt trips him hard core.
- As Rex later reports, shortly after Charles's departure she found out that Samgrass was a fake and that Cordelia was also sneaking Sebastian booze. She regretted having yelled at Charles.
- Lady Marchmain warns her daughter to stay away from Rex Mottram. When Julia and Rex get engaged, she tries to cover it up while she stalls and plots to drive them apart.

- She watches Rex's conversion with dismay, as he obviously doesn't take the process seriously, at least spiritually speaking.
- Lady Marchmain is devastated when Julia reports that she has been Rex's mistress for "some time now" and will continue to do so if they don't get married.
- She is further devastated when Julia and Rex are forced to marry under Protestant rites due to his prior marriage.
- Lady Marchmain falls ill. She wants to see Sebastian before she dies, but never gets a chance to.

Lord Marchmain Character Analysis

Until he comes home to Brideshead Castle to die, most of what Charles (and we) knows about Lord Marchmain is second hand. It starts with Anthony early in the novel, who tells the story of Marchmain's affair and his current exile from his wife and in fact all of England. Interestingly, Anthony takes Lord Marchmain's side and condemns Lady Marchmain.

Next we know, Sebastian explains that he's the only of his siblings maintaining any sort of real relationship with his father. Sebastian, too, sympathizes with his father, so for the second time Charles is inclined to side with Lord Marchmain and against Lady Marchmain. When Charles finally gets to meet the man, we once again get more information from a second-hand source than we do from our first-person narrator's observations. This time, it's Cara.

Cara's long description of Lord Marchmain's rocky relationship with his wife is there for a reason: it's one more step in Charles's education regarding love. It also sets up a parallel for us between Lord Marchmain's marriage to Lady Marchmain and Charles's "romantic friendship" with Sebastian. Both are first loves, as Cara says. Both are immature, and both act as forerunners to a later, more mature relationship. In the case of Lord Marchmain, this second love is presumably what he has with Cara.

Lord Marchmain is also a general parallel for Sebastian and his bad habits, as Lady Marchmain points out in the following passage:

"You see, it's all happened before. [...] I mean years ago. I've been through it all before with someone else whom I loved. Well, you must know what I mean – with his father. He used to be drunk in just that way. [...] But the running away – he ran away, too, you know. It was as you said just now, he was ashamed of being unhappy. Both of them unhappy, ashamed and running away. It's too pitiful."

Of course, Sebastian's character and decisions are very, very different from his father. He chooses suffering to be closer to God while Lord Marchmain essentially renounces his faith by moving to Italy and living with his mistress. That Lady Marchmain can't recognize these differences only suggests how little she understands her son.

Speaking of faith, let's look at what happens when Lord Marchmain comes back into the picture

at the end of Book Two. The first thing that Charles notices is that, actually, this guy is new kind of a jerk. "I had always been aware of a frame of malevolence under his urbanity," he says, "now it protruded like his own sharp bones through his skin." But it doesn't take long to figure out that Lord Marchmain's new personality is essentially just a reaction to his illness. He really, really doesn't want to die.

Now let's check out that death scene. By this point, Charles has tirelessly argued with Bridey and Cordelia and even Julia against having a priest come to perform the Last Sacrament on Lord Marchmain. "No one could have made it clearer," Charles says, "all his life, what he thought of religion. They'll come now, when his mind's wandering and he hasn't the strength to resist." Charles gets pretty worked up over the issue, and it is in fact the final dividing factor that destroys he and Julia's relationship. Charles comments that "the fate of more souls than one [is] at issue," and indeed this turns out to be true. Lord Marchmain decides not only if he will or will not see a priest, but also the heir to Brideshead and, in a way, whether or not Charles and Julia will stay together.

What does Lord Marchmain have to do with Charles and Julia's relationship? Plenty. When he – who all his life has opposed religion – manages to make the sign of his cross and willingly receive the Last Sacrament on his death bed, he brings Julia back to God. It is right after this touching scene that Julia decides she needs to accept God's love and break it off with Charles. She was inspired by her father's actions.

The other issue at hand is Charles's own conversion to Catholicism, which we talk about in "What's Up With the Ending?" The first time we see a shift in Charles's attitude toward Catholicism moments before Lord Marchmain's death, when they wait for him to accept or refuse the Last Sacrament. "I suddenly felt the longing for a sign," explains Charles, and after he sees it suddenly remembers a scene from the Bible. These are the first stirrings of what will ultimately lead to his position as a Catholic by the time he's in the army in the 1940s.

Lord Marchmain Timeline and Summary

- Anthony provides Charles with the back story on Lord Marchmain. She is a strict Catholic and Lord Marchmain converted in order to marry her. When he wanted a divorce, she refused on account of her religion. They are now separated and he lives in Venice with his mistress, Cara. He left his wife with everything – both Brideshead and Marchmain House and all the servants who went with them.
- Towards the end of their first summer together, Charles and Sebastian go to Venice to visit Lord Marchmain and Cara. Charles is surprised at how young Lord Marchmain appears and repeatedly calls him "Byronic."
- Charles gets more info from Cara. She says that Lord Marchmain's first love was Lady Marchmain, but that now he hates her and everyone who knows her. He can't even completely love Sebastian because he is Lady Marchmain's child. She claims this all stems from loving a woman before he was grown-up enough to do so.
- After Sebastian leaves Brideshead in a huff, Lady Marchmain takes Charles aside. She is

concerned about her son's depression, and explains that Lord Marchmain used to drink this same way – both men were ashamed of being unhappy.

- When Rex can't get Lady Marchmain's consent to marry Julia, he gets permission from Lord Marchmain instead. When Rex needs a Protestant ceremony instead of a Catholic one, Lord Marchmain again gives his consent.
- When Lord Marchmain is ill and dying, he decides to live out his final days at Brideshead. Charles is at first surprised by his new somewhat caustic attitude, but realizes that dying slowly has a profound effect on one's attitude.
- Lord Marchmain explains to Julia and Charles that he met and hates Beryl, Brideshead's new wife. He tells them he wants to leave Brideshead estate to the two of them, rather than to his eldest son.
- As Lord Marchmain lives out his final few months, he never wants to be alone, especially in the dark. He insists that at least one member of his family is around at all times.
- The doctor attending to Lord Marchmain explains to Charles that the man is afraid of dying.
- Julia, Bridey, Cordelia, Cara, Charles, and the doctor discuss whether or not Lord Marchmain should have a priest perform the Last Rites before his death. The first time they bring the priest in, Lord Marchmain refuses to see him. The second time, when he is very close to death and in fact barely conscious, Lord Marchmain does not protest (perhaps because he can't) and even gives a small sign of the cross.
- Lord Marchmain dies, leaving Brideshead to Julia in his will.

Mr. Ryder (Charles's Father) Character Analysis

Everything is subtext with Charles's father. Dry, sarcastic, and slightly mean subtext, but still. He's not around for many scenes in the novel, but his interactions with Charles are some of the novel's most memorable, and certainly most comic. Mr. Ryder spends most of his time reading alone in the library. We know he's a hermit because he made sure to "get rid of" Charles's Aunt Phillipa and because he seems to aim at getting rid of Charles as well. When he does emerge, it is for the purposes of eating formal dinners and taunting other people for his own amusement.

Despite these misanthropic characteristics, Mr. Ryder is far from dislikable and certainly no villain. On the contrary, he's more harmlessly amusing than anything else. In fact, the best way to think of Mr. Ryder is as a 1920s version of Dr. House. He's self-centered, gruff, and mocking – but he's hilarious and we all love him anyway.

Mr. Ryder allows for some great comparisons between Charles's home life and Sebastian's. While Sebastian has been utterly babied to death, Charles's father doesn't even care if he stays at Oxford or leaves:

"Then you agree to my leaving Oxford?"
"Agree? Agree? My dear boy, you're twenty-two."
"Twenty," I said, "twenty-one in October."
"Is that all? It seems much longer."

Sebastian can't seem to escape his family; Charles isn't even wanted at home. Sebastian greets his father with a kiss, and Charles notes that he himself "has not kissed [his] father since [he] left the nursery." The more we see of Sebastian's family, the more we are aware of the fundamental differences between his and Charles's upbringing.

Mr. Ryder (Charles's Father) Timeline and Summary

- After the Warden recommends that Mr. Ryder give his son 300 pounds a year as an allowance, Mr. Ryder deliberately gives him 550.
- Charles describes his father. He is about fifty, but appears to be seventy. He wears a formal smoking jacket to dinner and spends all day in the library instead of interacting with his son.
- Mr. Ryder joyfully torments his son about having run out of money early, without offering any solace or advice.
- Charles reveals some back-story: Mrs. Ryder died when he was young and his Aunt Phillipa – Mr. Ryder's sister – came to live with them. Mr. Ryder ultimately drove her out, as he says, leaving him to live his days alone in peace.
- Mr. Ryder amuses himself by pretending that Charles's very British friend is American and making snide-but-subtle comments to the man's face.
- Mr. Ryder designs dinner parties with guests designed specifically to irritate his son.
- When he finally meets Sebastian, Mr. Ryder finds him "very amusing."
- When Charles asks if it's OK for him to drop out of Oxford, Mr. Ryder responds that he's 22 and capable of making his own decisions (Charles is, in fact, 20).
- When Charles is preparing to divorce Celia, Mr. Ryder advises against it. He was under the impression that they were a happy couple, and also, thirty-four is too old to be getting divorced.

Anthony Blanche Character Analysis

Anthony Blanche is one of the most colorful characters you'll meet in Shmoop Literature. "A nomad of no nationality," "the aesthete par excellence," and a "fine piece of cookery," Anthony practically leaps off the pages of *Brideshead Revisited* with "colorful robes" and exaggerated, affected stutter. We can't really do much better than Charles's description of him "waxing in wickedness like a Hogarthian page boy," or disguising himself as a girl on account of a bet, dining with Proust, practicing black art in Cefalu, getting "cured of drug-taking in California and of an Oedipus complex in Vienna." Most telling is this line: "His vices flourished less in the pursuit of pleasure than in the wish to shock."

Indeed. In addition to being colorful and hilarious, Anthony is also flamboyantly and stereotypically gay. He threatens to "stick [Sebastian] full of barbed arrows like a p-p-pin-cushion" and says to Mulcaster, "Who knows better than you by taste for queer fish?"

He will later tell Sebastian, "If you want to be intoxicated there are so many much more delicious things [than alcohol]" while bringing him to who is most likely a male prostitute (though we could be way off here – who knows). He tells a group of mocking students that he would "like nothing better than the manhandled by you meaty boys." Sebastian later refers to him as "Charlus," a gay character from one of Proust's novels. Aside from innuendo, we have clear statements of his sexuality. "I may be inverted but I am not insatiable," he tells a group of young boys at his door. ("Inverted" was the not-so-politically correct term at the time for being gay.) Charles also refers to Sebastian as "my pansy friend" later in the novel.

Aside from the comedy, Anthony, much like Cara and Cordelia, is around in *Brideshead Revisited* to give Charles – and therefore the reader – information second hand. His relationship with Charles revolves around three key encounters, all of which consist of Anthony talking. A lot. First is the famous dinner out at Oxford, when Anthony puts in his two cents (make that two dollars) about the Flyte family. From his scathing critique of Julia as "a passionless, acquisitive, intriguing, ruthless killer" to his unexpected description of Sebastian as "insipid," Anthony has opinions on everything and everyone. His lengthy discourse with Charles serves as our introduction to the Flytes, and raises the stakes on the discoveries to follow. When Sebastian later dismisses these comments as gossip and lies, Charles writes them off. But Waugh makes sure we're still left wondering: Sebastian quickly changes the subject to that of his teddy-bear, just as Anthony suggested he would. Sounds like Blanche knows what he's talking about…

And indeed, many of Anthony's comments about the Flytes do turn out to be true. Julia is admittedly a semi-heathen like her brother, the history regarding Lord and Lady Marchmain's marriage is later confirmed, and Charles concludes that Lady Marchmain is as manipulative as everyone says. But what about Sebastian? Does Anthony's description hold true? Let's take a closer look at what he claims about our favorite teddy-bear-toting student:

"Tell me candidly, have you ever heard Sebastian say anything you have remembered for five minutes? You know, when I hear him talk, I am reminded of that in some ways nauseating picture of 'Bubbles.' […] When dear Sebastian speaks it is like a little sphere of soapsuds drifting off the end of an old clay pipe, anywhere, full of rainbow light for a second and then – "phut! – vanished, with nothing left at all, nothing."

OK…so Anthony has a point. Sebastian isn't exactly profound, and he tends spend most of his time talking about the temper of his stuffed bear. But what's wrong with simply being light-hearted? Plenty, according to Anthony. He believes that Sebastian poses a particular threat to Charles, and more specifically to Charles's artistic abilities.

In Charles's "Character Analysis" we talk a lot about Charles's aesthetic education and the progress he makes, artistically, throughout the course of the novel. Anthony and his comments on "English charm" are a big part of this education. He touches on the subject briefly during this first big speech at Oxford, but it's not until his final scene in the novel – out with Charles after the big exhibition – that the point really hits home for Charles (and for the reader, of course). Take a look:

"I was right years ago – more years, I am happy to say, than either of us shows – when I warned you. I took you out to dinner to warn you of charm. I warned you expressly and in great

detail of the Flyte family. *Charm is the great English blight. It does not exist outside these damp islands. It spots and kills anything it touches. It kills love; it kills art; I greatly fear, my dear Charles, it has killed you."*

While everyone else is going gaga over Charles's new, feral paintings, Anthony is unconvinced that Charles has managed to escape British charm and become a true artist. He says of the artwork: "It reminded me of dear Sebastian when he liked so much to dress up in false whiskers. It was charm again, my dear, simple, creamy English charm, playing tigers." Charm has strangled (or even "thwarted," an important word in *Brideshead Revisited*) Charles's artistic potential.

And of course, Anthony blames Sebastian for siccing this charm on Charles. Over and over again the word is used to describe Sebastian and his "Bubbles"-like manner of speaking. In just his first conversation with Charles, Anthony says that "Sebastian has charm […], *such* charm," suggests that in a church confessional he was "just being charming through the grille," reiterates that "he has such charm" and that "[he's] *so* charming, *so* amusing," claims that "those who are charming [like Sebastian] don't need brains," calls him "a little bundle of charm," concludes that in fact *all* the Flytes are "charming, of course," and finishes by saying "there was really very little left for poor Sebastian to do except be sweet and charming." He says the only reason Sebastian still visits is father is "because he's so charming," and advises that Charles not blame Sebastian for being "insipid," "simple," and… "charming."

OK. We think we've made our point. But now you can understand that when Anthony says "It is not an experience I would recommend for An Artist at the tenderest stage of his growth, to be strangled with charm" that what he's really warning Charles against isn't just good manners; *he's warning him against Sebastian* . And he might be right to do so. Consider the fact that Charles is a Captain in the army telling his story and seems to have abandoned art altogether. In fact, Charles straight out agrees with Anthony's interpretation of his paintings as "British charm playing tigers." "You're quite right," he says to Anthony, and that's the last we hear from him in the subject of art. When Lord Marchmain asks him at the end of the novel whether he will become an Artist, his response is simple, "No. As a matter of fact I am negotiating now for a commission in the Special Reserve." And that's that.

Anthony Blanche Timeline and Summary

- Charles meets Anthony when he's introduced to Sebastian's rather eccentric group of friends. Anthony recites passages from *The Wasteland* at the top of his lungs on Sebastian's balcony. He also takes a great liking to Charles.
- Jasper advises Charles against spending time with Anthony.
- Charles calls Anthony "a nomad of no nationality." He had a peculiar upbringing in a variety of locations all over the world, where he met and became close with the most famous of writers, philosophers, and thinkers. He's done and seen everything.
- Anthony takes Charles out to dinner. He tells a story about Boy Mulcaster and his friends harassing him and his own outlandish replies to their taunting. He talks about how

charming Sebastian is and always was.

- Anthony knows that Sebastian is a budding artist and encourages him in this endeavor.
- Then he dishes about Sebastian's family one by one. Personally, for all the Flyte charm he possesses, Anthony finds Sebastian to be insipid, like the "Bubbles" painting.
- Anthony then claims to have had an affair with a Duchess names Stefanie. He says that Sebastian is like her – enticing until he becomes a habit. He warns Charles not to be "strangled" by Sebastian's charm. He predicts that Sebastian will deny everything he's said and talk about his bear to change to subject; both these come to pass.
- When Charles and Sebastian return to Oxford for their second year, they find that Anthony Blanche is no longer there. It seems he has "formed an attachment" to a policeman in Munich.
- While traveling through Europe with Mr. Samgrass, Sebastian bumps into Anthony Blanche in Beirut.
- Years later (in 1926), Charles bumps into Anthony Blanche and Boy Mulcaster in London. Anthony fills him in on Sebastian.
- Years later, Anthony shows up at Charles's art exhibition for his South American paintings. He was excited at the prospect of seeing a few barbaric paintings, but he's now convinced that the images are nothing more than "simple, creamy English charm, playing tigers." He's also heard about Charles's affair with Julia, as has the rest of the world, apparently.

The Earl of Brideshead Character Analysis

Brideshead is an unusual and unique individual with "a gravity and restraint" beyond his years. Anthony describes him as "something archaic, out of a cave that's been sealed for centuries." He doesn't have Julia or Sebastian's good looks, in fact "has the face as though an Aztec sculptor had attempted a portrait of Sebastian." He also shares none of Sebastian's youthful verve nor his ability to charm – Brideshead doesn't even like to drink!

He also has his own method of thinking, speaking, and understanding things, a method which isolates him from others and makes communication, particularly between Charles and him, nearly impossible. Brideshead seems to recognize this: "It's something in the way my mind works I suppose. I have to turn a thing round and round, like a piece of ivory in a Chinese puzzle, until – click! – it fits into place – but by that time it's upside down to everyone else." And so does Charles, who concludes from their first debate on religion that "this disagreement was not a matter of words only, but expressed a deep and impassable division between us; neither had any understanding of the other, nor ever could."

This proves to be very true, particularly by the end of the novel when Charles is shacked up with Julia and Brideshead is planning to marry an ugly, over-the-hill widow. Brideshead unfortunately applies his own weird brand of logic and concludes that it's perfectly reasonable to call his sister out for being a sinful strumpet, essentially (our words, not Brideshead's). Brideshead is so caught up in logic and rules that he doesn't even comprehend the hurt he caused his sister by saying as much:

"Bridey, what a bloody offensive thing to say to Julia!"
"There was nothing she should object to. I was merely stating a fact well known to her."

OK, so he's apparently devoid of people skills. (No danger of being charmed to death here.) How did Brideshead get this way? For the umpteenth time, we turn to Cordelia for answers:

"If you haven't a vocation it's no good however much you want to be; and if you have a vocation, you can't get away from it, however much you hate it. Bridey thinks he has a vocation and hasn't. I used to think Sebastian had and hated it – but I don't know now He's as doomed as Sebastian."

She later says that "there are […] people who can't quite fit in either to the world or the monastic rule," and it would seem that Brideshead is one of them. He's obsessed with religion but never became a priest. He was left in the world with essentially nothing to do, and so became a bit of a farce – he ends up collecting matchboxes for a living. Look at what Charles has to say:

He had been completely without action in all his years of adult life; the talk of his going into the army, and into Parliament, and into a monastery, had all come to nothing. […] He was usually preposterous yet seldom quite absurd. He achieved dignity by his remoteness and agelessness; he was still half-child, already half-veteran; there seemed no spark of contemporary life in him; he had a kind of massive rectitude and impermeability, an indifference to the world, which compelled respect. Though we often laughed at him, he was never wholly ridiculous; at times he was even formidable.

It's clear that Brideshead never becomes an entirely comic figure, probably because he's too much of a tragedy – and too much a reminder of Sebastian's own "doomed" predicament.

The Earl of Brideshead Timeline and Summary

- Anthony describes Brideshead as "archaic" and a "learned bigot."
- While staying at Brideshead with Sebastian, Charles meets Bridey. He finds him to be particularly grave and stuffy. Brideshead is very religious and debates the ins and outs of the value of Catholicism with Charles over dinner. Charles concludes that they will never see the world from each other's point of view.
- Brideshead doesn't so much to help with Sebastian's alcoholism – he simply says that you can't stop people from doing what they want to do.
- Brideshead is present at the estate over Christmas. He takes Sebastian out hunting only to have him ditch the party to go drinking at hotel bar.
- While the family tries to figure out what to do about Sebastian's alcoholism, Charles talks with Brideshead and concludes that no one could ever want to be a Catholic after hearing what Bridey has to say.
- Bridey is the one to find out about Rex's first marriage. He declares that Julia's wedding is off.

- When Charles comes back from visiting a sick Sebastian in French Morocco, he meets with Brideshead and the two of them devise a plan for Sebastian to get living money while abroad.
- Cordelia later tells Charles that Brideshead always wished he had a vocation but never did.
- Brideshead reports to Charles and Julia that he met a wife through his new match-box collecting hobby. Her name is Beryl Muspratt and she is an unattractive, large widow with three children.
- He then wildly insults Julia and her decision to "live in sin" with Charles. Brideshead is unfazed when Charles calls him on being a jerk.
- Bridey tells Julia that he and Beryl want to move into Brideshead, which means she and Rex will have to move out.
- When Lord Marchmain comes to Brideshead castle to die, Brideshead is there to greet to him.
- Lord Marchmain reports that after meeting Beryl, he so disliked his son's choice of wife that he plans to leave his rightful inheritance – Brideshead Castle – to Julia instead.
- Brideshead soon realizes he isn't wanted and leaves, but he comes back when Lord Marchmain gets worse.
- Bridey is adamant that is father have a priest perform the Last Rites before he dies. After some heated debate he brings a priest, whom Lord Marchmain refuses. However, when he brings the priest back later, when Lord Marchmain is really ill, the old man accepts him and even gives a sign of the cross.

Lady Cordelia Flyte Character Analysis

If you've read any of our other "Character Analyses," you know by now that Cordelia is one wise old bird – especially considering that she's a child for the majority of *Brideshead Revisited*. Cordelia seems to answer all our big analytical questions: Why is Sebastian unhappy? What will happen to him in the end? What's the deal with Brideshead? Why do people hate Lady Marchmain? Amazingly, Cordelia addresses all of these questions – and she always does so while stuffing her face with eggs or meringue or appetizers at the Ritz. The point is that she's not pondering the fate or psychology of her siblings; she just happens to notice with her childlike curiosity the answers to questions plaguing the adults around her.

And thank goodness, because we'd be stuck on those study questions without her. In addition to being The Wisest Kid Ever, Cordelia is also the most loving and innocent of all the Flyte children. She's the only one of Sebastian's siblings who actually loves him, the same way that Charles does. Brideshead and Julia treat his alcoholism with mild annoyance, but Cordelia, unable to bear the sight of his suffering, sneaks him booze – just like Charles does. When she tells Charles to give Sebastian "her *special* love," she's likely referring to the fact that her love is genuine and therefore unique among her family members. She will later tell Charles that Julia "never loved [Sebastian] as [she and Charles] do," and also that she herself "loved [Sebastian] more than anyone." Her unconditional and lasting loyalty is so strong that it leaves even Charles feeling guilty at having abandoned his friend. "The word reproached me," he says; "there was no past tense in Cordelia's verb 'to love.'" It makes sense, then, that Cordelia is the character

given the privilege of describing her brother's death – see Sebastian's "Character Analysis" for more.

But enough about Sebastian; what happens to Cordelia herself? She grows from a spirited, youthful, exuberant, troublemaking child into a…well, Charles isn't exactly sure what she grows into. When he first sees her as an adult, he says, "It hurt to think of Cordelia growing up quite plain; to think of all that burning love spending itself […]. I thought her an ugly woman. […] When she said, 'It's wonderful to be home,' it sounded to my ears like the grunt of an animal returning to its basket." Ouch! But it's only pages later that he changes his mind: "As we sat there talking, and I saw Cordelia's fond eyes on all of us, I began to realize that she, too, had a beauty of her own." And yet, a mere couple of pages after that, Charles admits to Cordelia that he thinks of her as "thwarted."

So beautiful or not (and this determination probably has something to do with Charles's shifting definition of "beauty"), it's clear that Cordelia is yet another of the Flyte children caught in the tension between the secular world of happiness and the holy world of suffering. As a child, Cordelia hopes aloud that she has a vocation. "It means you can be a nun," she explains to our favorite agnostic. "If you haven't a vocation it's no good however much you want to be; and if you have a vocation, you can't get away from it, however much you hate it." We realize, then, by the end of the novel, that Cordelia doesn't have a vocation after all. She's figured this out, and explains to Charles that "there are […] people who can't quite fit in either to the world or the monastic rule. I suppose I'm something of the sort myself." Cordelia, then, is thwarted in more ways than one. Her holiness has been squandered as she has not fully devoted her life to God, yet her enthusiasm and charming trouble-making (as seen in her skillful imitations and practical jokes at Rex's expense) have been similarly wasted – she has, as Julia puts it, "grown up quite plain."

Lady Cordelia Flyte Timeline and Summary

- While Sebastian and Charles are sunbathing atop the roof, Cordelia comes clamoring up. She's eleven and talks about her pig, Francis Xavier.
- Charles hears that Cordelia is a troublemaker at her Catholic school.
- Despite Sebastian's reprimands, Cordelia refers to Charles by first name instead of calling him "Mr. Ryder." She tells Charles that she'll pray for him because he's agnostic.
- Cordelia tells Charles that she has six god-daughters in Africa which the nuns named after her for five schillings apiece.
- At Brideshead over Easter, Cordelia spills the beans to Lady Marchmain about Sebastian being drunk alone in his room.
- When Sebastian leaves to go to London, Cordelia tells Charles to give him "her *special* love."
- Cordelia is with the rest of the family and Samgrass at Brideshead after Christmas. When they discuss art, Cordelia asks Charles to confirm that modern art is "bosh." He does.
- After the hunting party, Cordelia comes back and reports that Sebastian has run to a hotel bar and gotten himself "in disgrace."

- After Charles gets a stern talking-to by Lady Marchmain and leaves Brideshead, he gets a letter from Cordelia. She reports that she's been supplying booze herself, that Rex and Julia are getting chummy (she disapproves), and that Samgrass has been found out and left. She adds that Rex is taking Sebastian to a doctor in Germany to try and do something about his alcoholism.
- When Rex is converting to Catholicism, Cordelia tells him all sorts of humorous lies about the dogma. He buys most of it, and she calls him a "chump."
- When Julia has her change-of-plans Protestant wedding, Cordelia is disappointed that she doesn't get to be a bridesmaid. She begs Julia not to get married and then tells her that she hopes she will be "always happy."
- When Lady Marchmain falls ill, Cordelia comes to London to take care of her in Marchmain House.
- When Charles is commissioned to paint Marchmain House, Cordelia comes by to watch. He takes her out to dinner at the Ritz. She is fifteen but, in his opinion, not as beautiful as Julia.
- Over dinner, they discuss Sebastian. Charles realizes that Cordelia knew more than he thought she did, and she professes that she loves her brother "more than anyone."
- They discuss religion; she explains that Sebastian and Julia are tied to religion forever, and that no matter how far they wander from it, they will always be brought back by "a twitch upon the thread" that holds them.
- She discusses her mother, explaining that people hated her when they wanted to hate God.
- She hopes she has a vocation so she can be a nun.
- Cordelia ends up a nurse in Spain.
- While Julia and Charles are living together at Brideshead, Cordelia comes by for a visit. She's 27 now. Julia says that she's grown up "quite plain," but Charles goes so far as to think her ugly when she arrives.
- When he watches Cordelia talk with her Nanny, however, he realizes she does have a beauty of her own.
- Cordelia updates Charles on Sebastian. She explains that she traveled to Tunis to find him and speak with The Superior.
- She explains that Sebastian is actually very holy. She believes that she and he are similar because they don't fit in to the real world, but they don't fit into the monastic world either.
- As Cordelia imagines Sebastian living his life out trying to be holy and falling back into drinking every now and then, she isn't worried. She thinks this isn't such a bad way of living, and adds that "no one is ever holy without suffering."
- Cordelia asks if Charles thought she was "thwarted" when he saw her for the first time after so many years. He says yes, and she responds that she thought the same thing about him and Julia.
- Cordelia stays at Brideshead with the rest of the family when her father comes there to die. He asks her to sit with him while he falls asleep, and she concludes that he is afraid of the dark.
- She sides with Bridey, adamantly insisting that her father gets a priest to perform the Last Rites.
- Cordelia is ultimately out of town on the night her father passes away.
- When Charles speaks with Nanny Hawkins in the epilogue, she tells him that Cordelia is abroad with Julia, helping with the war effort.

Mr. Samgrass of All Souls Character Analysis

Samgrass is the fly in the Oxford ointment. He's like long-distance parenting for Sebastian on behalf of Lady Marchmain. In short, he spoils all the good alcoholic fun while the boys are away at school. But perhaps worst of all is Samgrass's deluded idea that he is friends with Charles and Sebastian. Charles is not a happy camper after the Old Hundredth incident:

For the rest of that term he haunted us. Now that we were gated we could not spend our evenings together, and from nine o'clock onwards were alone and at Mr. Samgrass's mercy. Hardly an evening seemed to pass but he called on one or the other of us. He spoke of "our little escapade" as though he, too, had been in the cells, and had that bond with us.

Aside from being a complete buzz-kill ('90s slang of the day!), Samgrass is a great example of Lady Marchmain's ability to essentially own people. The first time Charles asks, "Who is Mr. Samgrass of All Souls?", Sebastian's immediate response is, "Just someone of Mummy's." This proves to be very true. Lady Marchmain has Samgrass by the you-know-what, and though we never directly see her telling him what to do, it's clear from his actions at Oxford that he's operating strictly at her beck and call. What's in it for Samgrass? As Charles says, "he was someone of almost everyone's who possessed anything to attract him." Samgrass likes to schmooze with the wealthy and aristocratic, and Lady Marchmain is right up his alley.

Now, one last interesting point. As it turns out, Waugh based the character of Mr. Samgrass on a professor of his at Oxford named Maurice Bowra. Looks like the bonus in writing a novel is getting to satirize all those profs you didn't like in college.

Mr. Samgrass of All Souls Timeline and Summary

- Samgrass is Lady Marchmain's way of keeping an eye on her son while he's at Oxford. He's also helping her out with her memorial book about her brother Ned. According to Charles, he spends his life sifting through archived documents and knowing everything there is to know about aristocratic families. Charles finds him to be very different from Lady Marchmain.
- When Sebastian is on trial for drunk driving, Samgrass gives a character testimonial in his favor that is probably what keeps him out of jail.
- Unfortunately for Sebastian, this fiasco leaves Samgrass thinking that they're buddies, even while he's disciplining him and Charles.
- While talking of his time at Brideshead, Samgrass mentions Boy's sister, Celia.
- Mr. Samgrass tells Charles not to plan on boarding with Sebastian at Oxford, since Lady Marchmain wants him to live with Monsignor Bell.
- When Lady Marchmain pulls Sebastian from Oxford, she sends him to stay with his father in Venice and then travel around Europe with Mr. Samgrass.
- Samgrass brings Sebastian to Brideshead two days after Christmas. He pretends that

everything went fine on their trip, but Charles knows something is up.
- It finally comes out: Samgrass lost Sebastian, who went off on an unchaperoned drinking binge.
- After he leaves Brideshead himself, Charles finds out that Samgrass was outed by Julia as a fake and left the estate as well.

Rex Mottram Character Analysis

It's easy to see why Julia is drawn to Rex. He's a bit older and more mature than the boys she's dated, he's well-off, he's mysterious, politically connected, lavishes her with ornate gifts, and drives her around everywhere she wants to go. She gets to treat him with both possession and disdain and he still worships at her feet. And then there's the icing on the cake – her mother doesn't like him. Talk about the perfect guy!

But even before Julia knows the real Rex, as readers we suspect that something's up. Waugh is careful not to let us like this guy too much. First of all, he's irritating. He's that super-capable but obnoxiously-loud guy who will bail you out of jail in the middle of the night but "rejoice in his efficiency" while doing so. Even Charles feels that "in his kindest moments Rex display[s] a kind of hectoring zeal as if he were thrusting a vacuum cleaner on an unwilling housewife." Rex also seems to have no shame about carrying on an affair with the married socialite Brenda Champion, even while he's wooing Julia. He also treats his potential marriage as a business arrangement. As Charles says of Rex, "He wanted a woman; he wanted the best on the market, and he wanted her cheap; that was what it amounted to."

And it's all downhill after the engagement. Rex treats Julia's religion without respect, converting without thought or effort and trying to replace sincerity with money ("All right then, I'll get an annulment. What does it cost? Who do I get it from? Has Father Mowbray got one?"). We hear the tragic tale of their marriage only years after the wedding (which Julia calls a "gruesome affair" in itself). As she explains, Rex started up again with Brenda Champion only months after their honeymoon. Charles notes that his political welfare has gone downhill considerably, too, as he made some questionable friends, "flirt[ed] with communists and fascists," and was all around a "vaguely suspect" character.

But most disconcerting is Julia's repeated claim that "Rex isn't anybody at all. […] He just doesn't exist." In a way, Rex suffers from the same lack of people skills that so define Julia's brother Brideshead (see his "Character Analysis" for more). He has "the faculties of a man highly developed," as Julia says, but he doesn't understand human emotions. This explains why he is able to treat proposing to Julia as a business arrangement, why he doesn't care that their baby was born dead simply because she was a daughter and not a son, why he doesn't understand why his wife is upset at his affair with Brenda, and why he seems to not really care that his wife is cheating on him. He's not even angry with Charles for the affair! All he says is, "If I've been around too much, just tell me, I shan't mind." Even when Julia is readying to divorce him, Rex is concerned with politics, not love. With casual annoyance he tells Charles that "there's too much going on altogether at the moment […] and I've got a lot on my mind. […]

If Julia insists on a divorce, I suppose she must have it. […] But she couldn't have chosen a worse time. Tell her to hang on a bit, Charles, there's a good fellow." It looks like Julia's assessment is largely correct: "Rex isn't a real person at all."

Rex Mottram Timeline and Summary

- Julia visits Sebastian and Charles at Oxford and brings Rex with her. He and Julia invite them to a ball that night.
- When Sebastian, Charles, and Boy are arrested, they call Rex to help them with their jail situation. He does.
- Rex arrives at Brideshead a few days after Christmas with a present for Julia: a live tortoise with her initials in the shell in diamonds.
- Rex proposes that, as a solution to Sebastian's alcoholism, he take him to this guy he knows in Zurich.
- Cordelia later reports to Charles that Rex and Julia are getting very close, much to her dismay.
- Rex comes to visit Charles in Paris and takes him out to dinner. He gives the latest news from Brideshead and discusses his intentions to marry Julia and the barriers in his way (namely Lady Marchmain). He admits to his affair with Brenda Champion.
- Rex is very picky regarding the cognac they are served after dinner.
- In May, his engagement to Julia is announced. In June they are quickly and quietly married.
- Charles gives us the back-story on Rex and Julia. Julia liked the fact that he was older than she, and that he was a somewhat unsavory character. They met when Rex was staying with Brenda in France and Julia was nearby with her aunt. He was getting bored and so decided to pursue Julia as a project of sorts.
- As Rex showered Julia with more and more gifts, she grew dependent on him and finally fell in love. One evening, he flaked on her and spent the night with Brenda instead. The next morning, Julia was upset and agreed to marry him, since being engaged was the only way to justify her anger.
- They start fooling around together, until Julia puts an end to it on the grounds of her being a Catholic. Rex gets it elsewhere, from Brenda.
- Julia, in an attempt to keep Rex faithful to her, resumes the fooling around and essentially renounces her religion in the process.
- Lady Marchmain keeps trying to keep the engagement a secret, but Rex eventually gets Lord Marchmain's consent, which is enough.
- Now Rex has to convert to Catholicism. He does so, but fails to treat the conversion with the appropriate gravity. He also buys all of Cordelia's ridiculous stories about Catholic dogma.
- When Brideshead announces that Rex has been married before, Rex doesn't think it's a big deal. He insists he'll just get an annulment and it takes some time for the Flytes to convince him that it doesn't work like that.
- He and Julia decide to get married in a Protestant church.
- Julia later remarks that Rex isn't a complete human being, and that the priest who tried to

convert him was the only one to really understand this.

- Aboard the ship on the Atlantic, Julia gives Charles some more detail. She and Rex tried to have a baby, but it was born dead. He didn't mind so much because it was a girl anyway. She again says that, though Rex isn't "intentionally unkind," "he isn't a real person at all."
- She adds that he went back to sleeping with Brenda Champion about two months after their honeymoon was over.
- Julia explains that she is now living with Rex at Brideshead. He is disappointed with her and writes her off completely until someone he thinks is important takes a liking to her. She feels she's being punished for marrying him.
- Charles joins Julia and Rex at Brideshead, with a group of Rex's loud and obnoxious friends.
- When it comes out that both Charles and Julia want divorces, Rex asks Charles to get his divorce but leave Julia alone. Charles knows that Rex's life isn't going well, as he's played his political cards the wrong way and has gotten some bad press.
- Julia officially divorces Rex.

Boy Mulcaster Character Analysis

Boy Mulcaster is essentially an ill-mannered rich kid. When Anthony tells the story of him and his friends in colored tailcoats threatening to throw him in Mercury, we know that Boy has just come from some pretentious dining establishment, is now drunk, and is terrorizing the campus and causing trouble. Anthony quickly fills in the details when he tells Charles, "If you want to know what a real degenerate is, look at Boy Mulcaster." It seems that Boy, who is apparently a British Lord, made a general fool of himself while staying with Anthony as a guest. Anthony's opinion of Boy is confirmed when we see him pull a fire alarm at a crowded nightclub because he simply wants to "cheer things up." It just goes to show that being from the upper class doesn't necessarily mean you have any class.

And aside from that little platitude, Mulcaster simply serves the plot purpose of bringing Celia into the picture for Charles to eventually marry.

Boy Mulcaster Timeline and Summary

- Over dinner, Anthony Blanche tells Charles about one night when a group of boys – among them Boy Mulcaster – tried to put him in Mercury. He refers to him as a "real degenerate."
- Rex and Julia invite Charles, Sebastian, and Boy to a party. At Boy's suggestion, they leave to go to an old joint of his, the Old Hundredth. They get drunk and are later arrested for drunk driving.
- When Charles comes back to London in 1926, he goes out to dinner with Anthony Blanche and Boy Mulcaster. Boy gets bored and pulls the fire alarm.
- Celia explains that Boy was going to marry a girl, but pulled out at the last minute.

- When Charles works out his divorce from Celia with Boy, he doesn't seem too upset about his sister. He even tells Charles that he always had a soft spot for Julia.

Celia Mulcaster Character Analysis

Charles keeps us in the dark for ages about the identity of his wife. He doesn't even officially clue his reader into the fact that he's married; he just casually mentions that he has a wife and expects us to fill in the details. Finally we realize – through hearing her speak her own name over the telephone – that Mrs. Ryder is in fact Celia, Boy Mulcaster's sister.

If you missed her introduction earlier in the novel, it's understandable. We get only a brief second-hand description, courtesy of Mr. Samgrass:

"I shall miss the pretty creatures about the house – particularly one Celia; she is the sister of our old companion in adversity, Boy Mulcaster, and wonderfully unlike him. She has a bird-like style of conversation, pecking away at the subject in a way I find most engaging, and a school-monitor style of dress which I can only call 'saucy.'"

Remember that Charles is narrating this all in retrospect. The fact that he passes over this moment without the least bit of attention or care is a real indication of his feelings for his wife: complete apathy at best, utter disdain at the worst. (For comparison, think about the pages and pages Charles devotes to describing Julia's every word and movement, even long before they get involved in Book Two.)

We can certainly confirm this assessment of Charles's marriage when we see it first-hand aboard the ship on the Atlantic, based on his descriptions of his wife (whose name he still refuses to use). "[She] was adept in achieving such small advantages," he says of their large rooms on the ship, "first impressing the impressionable with her chic and my celebrity and, superiority once firmly established, changing quickly to a pose of almost flirtatious affability." She references Charles's proposal to her, and his response is, "As I remember, *you* popped [the question]." He resentfully describes her attempt to "ingratiate" him with "two Hollywood magnates" she invited to the party which he seems to resent in itself.

This is really some brilliant characterization on Waugh's part. Charles is never deliberately antagonistic towards his wife, but it's painfully clear that he in no way loves her. He doesn't even want to see their children! Just as Lord Marchmain "can barely be happy with Sebastian because he is [Lady Marchmain's] son," so Charles can not be happy with his children, because they belong to a woman he hates. (There's also a possibility that Charles's first child, Johnjohn, isn't his, since we find out that Celia has not been faithful.)

But is Charles's disdain warranted? What's so bad about Celia? She's certainly nothing like Julia, that's for sure. Read about this "Foil" in Shmoop's "Character Role ID" and you'll see what we're talking about. Julia is smart, tough, and a formidable match for Charles, while Celia is overly-feminine and charming to the point of annoyance. In fact, Celia represents everything

Anthony so vehemently warned Charles against – "creamy British charm." Charles recognizes this himself. When his wife speaks with her calm, aristocratic, charming way, he confesses that "throughout [his] married life, again and again, [he has] felt [his] bowels shrivel within [him] at the things she said." In fact, he doesn't feel free of her charm until he "detects [her] in adultery." It's almost as though she proved herself to be – like her brother – rather a degenerate, NOT the picture of perfect British charm after all. Conveniently, this gives Charles moral permission –at least in his mind – to pursue Julia without compunction.

Kurt Character Analysis

Kurt is Sebastian's German friend whom he takes up with once he leaves England. We first hear of Kurt through Anthony (what else is new), who describes him as "a great clod of a German who'd been in the Foreign Legion" and "got out by shooting off his great toe." Sebastian apparently "found him starving" and took him in like a stray cat.

Once Charles finally meet this character, it's clear that Anthony wasn't too far off the mark; Kurt is unattractive, dislikable, and altogether cringe-inducing. Charles notes his "wolfish look" and "unnaturally lined" face, that "one of his front teeth [is] missing" and that those "teeth he had were stained with tobacco and set far apart." Yet his defining physical feature seems to the pus oozing out of his injured foot. (Grimace now.) He's lounging in a chair and drinking beer brought to him by the servant Sebastian pays for. He seems utterly unconcerned that his friend is ill and in the hospital, and his main worry is that Charles convince Lady Marchmain, who he knows is dying, to send more money.

Amazingly enough, Sebastian is completely aware of Kurt's shortcomings. He tells Charles to arrange his finances so that he gets a limited allowance every week and only when he "ha[s] a proper use for it." "Otherwise," explains Sebastian, "Kurt will get me to sign off on the whole lot when I'm tight and then he'll go off and get into all kinds of trouble." Then here's The Big Question: why in the world is Sebastian friends with a man who's milking him for everything he's got?

You might suspect that lust has something to do with it, that Sebastian is engaged in a sexual relationship with Kurt. But Brideshead asks Charles this very thing when he says, "Do you consider that there is anything vicious in my brother's connection with this German?" ("Vicious" is yet another outdated, politically incorrect word for "gay.") Charles answers definitively that he is sure this is not the case. "It's simply […] two waifs coming together," he says.

But it is Sebastian who very fully answers this big question for us (and for Charles), in this oh-so important passage, which we're sure by now you have all underlined, highlighted, and dog-eared to death like good, aggressive readers:

"You know, Charles, it's rather a pleasant change when all your life you've had people looking after you, to have someone to look after yourself. Only of course it has to be someone pretty hopeless to need looking after by me."

This raises some interesting question regarding the nature of Sebastian's earlier relationship with Charles. As he says in the hospital in Morocco, "I won't ask if you like Kurt; no one does. It's funny – I couldn't get on without him, you know." Sebastian may be taking care of Kurt, but he's entirely dependent upon him. Sebastian needs someone to take care of, which makes us wonder if that's what Charles was all about for him back at Oxford. After all, we know that Sebastian took over as Charles's aesthetic teacher (see each of their "Character Analyses" for more) and introduced him to the "enchanted garden" of his acquaintances and lifestyle in college. Has Sebastian simply replaced Charles with Kurt, or are these two very different kinds of relationships? Take it away, Shmooper.

Hooper Character Analysis

Ryder's new platoon commander.

Lunt Character Analysis

Charles's servant at Oxford.

Hardcastle Character Analysis

The man from whom Sebastian borrows a car. Repeatedly.

Jasper Character Analysis

Charles's overbearing cousin, who attends Oxford and is a few years older than Charles.

Mr. Collins Character Analysis

Mr. Collins is one of Charles's first term friends at Oxford.

Mr. Partridge Character Analysis

Mr. Partridge is one of Charles's first term Oxford friends.

Hobson Character Analysis

Hobson is Sebastian's servant at Oxford.

Duc de Vincennes Character Analysis

Duc de Vincennes is the man whose wife (Stefanie) Anthony claims to have had a thing with.

Stefanie Character Analysis

The Duchess Anthony claims to have had a thing with.

Sir Adrian Porson Character Analysis

Sir Adrian Porson is a pet and an acquaintance of Lady Marchmain.

Monsignor Bell Character Analysis

One of Lady Marchmain's people at Oxford. Monsignor Bell terrorizes Sebastian.

Hayer Character Analysis

Hayer is a servant at the Ryder home.

Melchior Character Analysis

Charles's cousin. Melchior once ran out of money and had to run to Australia, or so Mr. Ryder claims.

Mrs. Abel Character Analysis

Mrs. Abel is the cook at the Ryder home.

Phillipa Character Analysis

Mr. Ryder's sister. Phillipa lived with her brother and Charles after Charles's mother died.

Jorkins Character Analysis

One of Charles's boyhood friends.

Sir Cuthbert Character Analysis

An old friend and dinner guest of Mr. Ryder's. His presence is designed specifically to torment Sebastian.

Lady Orme-Herrick Character Analysis

An old friend and dinner guest of Mr. Ryder's. Her presence is designed specifically to torment Sebastian.

Miss Gloria Orme-Herrick Character Analysis

An old friend and dinner guest of Mr. Ryder's. Her presence is designed specifically to torment Sebastian.

Wilcox Character Analysis

The butler at Brideshead Castle.

Father Phipps Character Analysis

A priest that comes by Brideshead estate during the summer.

Francis Xavier Character Analysis

Cordelia's pig.

Plender Character Analysis

Lord Marchmain's valet in Venice.

Ned Character Analysis

Lady Marchmain's deceased brother.

Fanny Rosscommon Character Analysis

Lady Marchmain's sister-in-law. Julia later refers to her as her aunt, Lady Rosscommon.

Borethus Character Analysis

Borethus is the guy Rex knows in Zurich who can supposedly cure alcoholism.

Charlie Kilcartney Character Analysis

Charlie Kilcartney is the guy that Borethus supposedly cured of alcoholism.

The Strickland-Venables Character Analysis

The neighboring family to the Flytes.

Brenda Champion Character Analysis

Rex's bit o' stuff (or mistress).

Father Mowbray Character Analysis

The priest who converts Rex to Catholicism so he can marry Julia.

Aunt Betty Character Analysis

One of Cordelia's aunts.

Sarah Evangeline Cutler Character Analysis

Rex's first wife.

Jean de Brissac la Motte Character Analysis

The fake name of a "Belgian futurist" who hangs out with Charles and his friends during the spring of 1926 in London.

Nada Alopov Character Analysis

One of Anthony's friends in Marseilles, who provides something "more intoxicating" than alcohol. Maybe a male prostitute, maybe a drug dealer…

Jean Luxmore Character Analysis

One of Anthony's friends who visits this Alopov character.

Bill Meadow Character Analysis

Charles and Boy join Meadow's flying squad in London.

Johnjohn Character Analysis

Celia and Charles's son.

Caroline Character Analysis

Celia and Charles's daughter.

Bertha Van Halt Character Analysis

Caroline Ryder's godmother.

Sir Joseph Emden Character Analysis

The architect commissioned by Celia to turn the barn into a studio for Charles.

Mrs. Stuyvesant Oglander Character Analysis

One of the guests at Celia's party aboard the ship. Later Mrs. Stuyvesant Oglander turns out to be a friend of Anthony Blanche's mother.

Mr. Kramm Character Analysis

The Hollywood man at Celia's party.

Senator Stuyvesant Oglander Character Analysis

The Senator sits with Charles and Celia at the Captain's table at dinner aboard the ship.

Margot Character Analysis

A friend of Celia's who throws a party after Charles's private exhibition.

Tom Character Analysis

The man who hits on Charles and/or Anthony at the seedy bar.

Grizel Character Analysis

A woman who keeps company with Rex and his crowd; Charles calls her a "rake."

Beryl Muspratt Character Analysis

Brideshead's eventual wife.

Robin Character Analysis

Celia's rebound boyfriend after her separation from Charles.

The Superior Character Analysis

The head monk at the monastery in Tunis which takes in Sebastian.

Father Mackay Character Analysis

The priest Brideshead gets to give his father the last rites.

The Quartering Commandant Character Analysis

The army officer who shows Charles around Brideshead estate in the novel's epilogue.

Character Roles

Protagonist
Charles Ryder
As the narrator and central character, Charles is definitely our protagonist here. We follow his story through trials of love, family, friendship, and education, and it is his character that we empathize with throughout all of *Brideshead Revisited*.

Guide/Mentor
Anthony Blanche
Surprised? Anthony is absent for most of the novel and manages to be drunk or in the process of getting there every time we see him, but he's a big part of Charles's aesthetic education, as we talk all about in "Character Analysis." Anthony is the one to warn Charles – rightly so – of the dangers of British charm – and he's also our guide to understanding the Flyte family.

Guide/Mentor
Cordelia Flyte
Cordelia's little nuggets of pre-pubescent wisdom help Charles to understand the Flytes and help the reader to understand the novel. Her insights on Lady Marchmain, Sebastian's alcoholism, and Bridey's religious predicament are among the most important in the novel.

Foil
Julia Flyte and Celia Ryder
We get the best comparison of these two women aboard the ship on the Atlantic, when together with Charles they form a neat little love triangle. Since Charles is married to but resents Celia and in love with Julia, the stage is set for nice little foil.

First, look at the dinner conversation when they're all seated at the Captain's table. Celia is thrilled to be a VIP; Julia gives Charles "a little dismal symbol of sympathy" – an emotion much

more in line with Charles's own opinion of the seating arrangements. While he and Julia banter cleverly about King Lear, Celia is left in the dark. "Don't [even] try to explain," she insists to them. If Julia is tom-boy masculine, Celia is delicate-flower feminine, with her "softness and English reticence, her very white, small, regular teeth, her neat rosy finger-nails [...] her peculiar charm." Notice that Julia is the only woman up and about during the storm with the men, while Celia lies in bed sick from the tossing seas. Everything that attracts Charles to Julia similarly explains why he could never be happy with a woman like Celia.

Character Clues

Everyone reacts differently to the same thing

Don't worry, we've got plenty of examples to keep you happy. Jump to Book One, Chapter Five when the gang is holed up at Brideshead for the holiday and Sebastian gets drunk alone in his room. Julia, who certainly never loves her brother the way Charles does, remarks, "How very peculiar! What a bore he is!" She adds that Charles "must deal with him," as "it's no business of [hers]." Cordelia, who is a child and doesn't understand the severity of the problem, simply giggles and recites the famous headline, "Marquis's Son Unused to Wine." Brideshead is as unfazed as his sister by Sebastian's clearly burgeoning alcoholism, remarking in an "odd, impersonal way" that it was an "extraordinary time" to drink and that "you can't stop people if they want to get drunk." On the other hand, Charles's concern for his friend is made clear by his concern and his request to everyone around him to help.

For another example, look at Book Two, Chapter Four when Charles readies for his divorce from Celia. Mulcaster is as cavalier as ever, remarking to the man leaving his sister that he "always had a soft spot for Julia" himself. Charles's father disregards his son's happiness entirely, claiming that "if [he] couldn't be happy with [Celia], why on earth should [he] expect to be happy with anyone else?" He takes the whole thing lightly and even advises Charles to "give up the whole idea." Rex is as selfish as ever; he doesn't care that Julia is stifled and unhappy, he just wants her to stay in the marriage because times are bad politically, socially, and financially. Of course, good old Nanny Hawkins, who loves from a haze of oblivion, says: "Well, dear, I hope it's all for the best."

Defining the Negative

We found a particularly interesting "characterization" moment at the very start of Book One, Chapter Five, right when Charles meets Lady Marchmain for the first time. Until now, we've heard only rumors and speculation about this woman, mostly from Anthony Blanche and of course from Sebastian himself. But now we're ready for Charles's big first impression. And what do we get? A full page description of Mr. Samgrass, a comparatively minor character. What gives? Well, AFTER characterizing Samgrass, the narrative reads: "He was with Lady Marchmain when I first met them, and I thought then that she could not have found a greater contrast to herself than this intellectual-on-the-make, nor a better foil to her own charm." So while the narrative doesn't directly characterize Sebastian's mother, it *indirectly* characterizes her by defining the man that Charles identifies as her complete opposite.

Hear it from other characters

Why should narrator Charles have to do all the characterization when the other characters do it for him? Anthony certainly does plenty of telling himself, namely in Chapter Two when he calls Julia "a *fiend* – a passionless, acquisitive, intriguing, ruthless killer," describes Lord Marchmain as "handsome, a *magnifico*, a voluptuary, Byronic, bored, infectiously slothful" and Brideshead as "archaic." Cara later provides Charles (and of course the reader) with a slew of information regarding both Lord Marchmain (in particular his relationship with his wife) and Sebastian (in particular his alcoholism). It is Julia who provides the vital piece of information on Rex, that "he isn't a real person at all, [...] simply isn't there," and surprisingly enough Celia who delivers the very important line, "Charles lives for one thing – Beauty."

Incredibly Telling Singular Lines
Sometimes a well-placed one-liner is all you need. For example…

This line expresses Lady Marchmain's manipulative cunning: "One was never summoned for a little talk, or consciously led to it; it merely happened, when she wished to speak intimately, that one found oneself alone with her."

Rex Mottram may be helpful, but he's too self-congratulatory to be liked. After he helps the guys out of jail for the night, this line is a solo paragraph: "It was plain that he rejoiced in his efficiency." And also, "In his kindest moments Rex displayed a kind of hectoring zeal as if he were thrusting a vacuum cleaner on an unwilling housewife."

Samgrass is…just…plain…dislikable: "[He had] the general appearance of being too often bathed" and "he was someone of almost everyone's who possessed anything to attract him."

Celia's wife, despite treating Charles with all the kindness in the world, is impossible to side with: "My wife was adept in achieving such small advantages, first impressing the impressionable with her chic and my celebrity and, superiority once firmly established, changing quickly to a pose of almost flirtatious affability." When they are plied with gifts after the storm on the Atlantic, she says, "How sweet people are," and Charles remarks that she "speaks as though the gale were a private misfortune of her own which the world in its love was condoling." This remark not only characterizes Celia, but Charles's feelings towards her (hint: it's not a good feeling).

Literary Devices

Symbols, Imagery, Allegory

The "Et in Arcadia Ego" Skull
We're referring to the slightly morbid dorm-room décor which Charles has lying around early in Book One. We might have missed it altogether if Waugh hadn't rather pointedly entitled Book One "Et in Arcadia Ego" and told us to look closer.

The phrase is Latin and *literally* translates to, "And in Arcadia I am." (The "to be" verb is

implied.) But it is most often translated to reflect its meaning and not just its words, in which case it reads, "Even in Arcadia I exist." ("Arcadia" is another word for a pastoral paradise.) The quote is famous as the title of this painting, but Waugh likely had this painting in mind instead. There are different ways to interpret the line. It could be that a dead person is speaking it — "even in Arcadia I existed," as in, "even though I'm dead now, I used to live happily in a paradise of green grasses and such," or it could be that death is speaking it, as in, "I'm around threatening to end your life even when you're in paradise."

This second one sure makes for an ominous reading of Book One of *Brideshead Revisited*. Charles is in Arcadia, but the threat of death (and the very tumultuous Book Two) is ever-present. Of course, considering that we get hints of Sebastian's depression and straight-up prophecies of his impending alcoholism every third page doesn't exactly help either. On the other hand, the first interpretation fits nicely with the image of Charles the narrator, now essentially 'dead' since he is loveless, childless, middle-aged, etc., looking back on the Arcadia in which he once existed.

The word "Arcadia" also has a religious connotation, which sadly we cannot ignore when talking about anything in *Brideshead Revisited*. Charles says that he "believed [him]self very near heaven during those languid days at Brideshead," so here is yet a third interpretation of the phrase, this time viewing "Arcadia" as a very specific paradise: heaven. Remember how we talked in "Character Analysis" about Charles using art to replace religion? Right, well here he is using youth to replace the Catholic concept of heaven. Lends a little support to that title addendum "the Sacred and Profane Memories," doesn't it?

The Crock of Gold

Another place to see this paradise/death dichotomy is in two passages from Book One. The first happens at the very start of Charles's flashback, when Sebastian says while picnicking, "[This is] Just the place to bury a crock of gold. [...] I should like to bury something precious in every place where I've been happy and then, when I was old and ugly and miserable, I could come back and dig it up and remember." Later, when Charles leaves Brideshead behind having "disappointed" Lady Marchmain by supplying her alcoholic son booze, he remarks: "As I drove away and turned back in the car to take what promised to be my last view of the house, I felt that I was leaving part of myself behind, and that wherever I went afterwards I should feel the lack of it, and search for it hopelessly, as ghosts are said to do, frequenting the spots where they buried material treasures without which they cannot pay their way to the nether world." This is quite a twist on Sebastian's original meaning. The "crock of gold" was initially a part of the beautiful Arcadian landscape of Charles's youth. But then it is the gold used to pay passage to the underworld. It's a lot like the image of a skull in the midst of a pastoral paradise. Oh, wait...

"That Low Door in the Wall"

Before his first luncheon with Sebastian (a peace offering after the puking incident), Charles pauses to consider whether or not he should go. He was uncertain, he says, "for it was foreign ground and there was a tiny, priggish, warning voice in my ear which [...] told me it was seemly to hold back." But look at his eventual reasoning for attending:

But I was in search of love in those days, and I went full of curiosity and the faint, unrecognized apprehension that here, at last, I should find that low door in the wall, which others, I knew, had

found before me, which opened on an enclosed and enchanted garden, which was somewhere, not overlooked by any window, in the heart of that grey city.

Enchanted garden…sounds a bit like "Arcadia," doesn't it? Charles certainly gets what he was looking for when he dives headfirst into this friendship with Sebastian. As we talk about in "Character Analysis," Sebastian truly does open up a whole new world for Charles – a world of youth, care-free days, wine, and, most importantly, of art and beauty.

But much later, when Sebastian has become an alcoholic and Lady Marchmain is angry with Charles for supplying him booze, Charles drives away from Brideshead for what he thinks will be the last time and remarks, "A door had shut, the low door in the wall I had sought and found in Oxford; open it now and I should find no enchanted garden." This is more of that paradise/death stuff we've talked so much about in regards to the phrase "Et in Arcadia Ego." That ever-present skull tainting the perfect pastoral landscape has brought to an end those "heavenly days at Brideshead."

The Twitch Upon the Thread
This is the title of Book Two and also a phrase we hear twice inside the text. The first occurrence comes at the end of Book One, when Charles is out to dinner with Cordelia at the Ritz:

"D'you know what Papa said when he became a Catholic? […] He said […]: 'You have brought back my family to the faith of their ancestors.' […] The family haven't been very constant [in regards to religion], have they? There's him gone and Sebastian gone and Julia gone. But God won't let them go for long, you know. I wonder if you remember the story Mummy read us the evening Sebastian first got drunk – I mean the bad evening. Father Brown said something like 'I caught him' (the thief) 'with an unseen hook and an invisible line which is long enough to let him wander to the ends of the world and still to bring him back with a twitch upon the thread.'"

Cordelia paints the image of God with essentially a fishing line tied to every Catholic. A given Catholic – like Julia, for example – might wander away from God, but God can pull on the thread (or give it a "twitch" in this case) and yank him right back at any time.

As the titles of Book One and Two of Brideshead suggest, Book One is the wandering away part and Book Two is when everyone gets yanked bank by the twitch. Sebastian wandered all the way to Northern Africa, but ended up where? At a monastery. Julia abandoned God and the sanctity of her marriage, but returns to her faith at the end of the novel. Lord Marchmain was never much for religion, but accepts the Last Sacrament on his death bed. Notice what Charles says when Lord Marchmain refuses the priest for the first time: "I felt triumphant. I had been right, everyone else had been wrong, truth had prevailed; the thread that I had felt hanging over Julia and me ever since that evening at the fountain had been averted, perhaps dispelled for ever." And notice Julia's very reason for breaking up with Charles is right in line with Cordelia's thread metaphor: "The worse I am, the more I need God," she says. "I can't shut myself out from His mercy."

Most surprising of all is the twitch upon the thread which brings Charles to Catholicism. But we talk about that in "What's Up With the Ending?"

Setting

England, from 1922 to the early 1940s

The prologue and epilogue of *Brideshead Revisited* take place during the early 1940s, in the midst of WWII. Charles's flashback – the main narrative comprising the novel – goes back to the 1920s and takes the reader forward through the following two decades. Brideshead Castle and the surrounding estate is of course at the center of the novel's setting, as it comes to represent all the novel's major themes and is of course the trigger for Charles's recollection. But you can read all about that in "What's Up With the Title?"

Narrator Point of View

First Person (Central Narrator)

Charles Ryder narrates two decades of his own memories over the course of *Brideshead Revisited*. We're allowed into the thoughts of the twenty-something Charles he recalls as well as the reflections of the forty-something man he is when the novel begins. In fact, it's sometimes hard to tell where one begins and the other ends. Charles admits that he's tempted to imbue his younger self with qualities and maturities he didn't actually have. He also openly admits to the unreliability of his memory. But, in a way, we actually trust Charles more on account of his openness. He's not trying to manipulate the reader at all; if anything, he is himself a victim of memory's manipulation.

Genre

Family Drama, Romance, Tragicomedy

Family seems to the source of everyone's problems in *Brideshead Revisited*. Familial conflict certainly drives the novel's plot and themes, from Lady Marchmain's machinations to Lord Marchmain's bitter resentment to Sebastian's impenetrable suffering. Charles's own story only begins once he becomes entrenched in the Flyte family web. If Charles's friendship with Sebastian dominates the first book of Brideshead, his romance with Julia controls the second. The ups and downs of their respective marriages, divorces, and of course their affair are at the core of the post half-time drama. As far as "tragicomedy" goes, Waugh manages to combine his wry, mocking sense of humor with the very serious subject matter of religion and lost love. Sebastian's end in Morocco and Charles's doomed love with Julia is no picnic, but at the same time the sarcastic commentary on war, society, and wealth keeps us smiling.

Tone

Wry, Nostalgic

The comic exchanges between Charles and his misanthropic father are some of the most famous in the novel, or even in Waugh's collective work. This type of sardonic humor pervades *Brideshead Revisited*. The novel ruthlessly satirizes the extravagance of the British aristocracy. Just look at Julia's diamond-studded tortoise and the reactions it provokes: Lady Marchmain wonders if it eats the same things as an ordinary tortoise, and Samgrass wants to know if they can stick another tortoise in the shell when it dies. You've also got "life-size effigy of a swan, moulded in ice and filled with caviar," a "chilly piece of magnificence," in Charles's words, "dripping at the beak." (Hilarious.) Waugh also mocks the careless attitudes of the spoiled rich, mostly through Boy Mulcaster, who rings a fire alarm one night in order to "cheer things up" at a boring nightclub.

But this wry wit it in constant balance with the novel's melancholy nostalgia. This sadness really hits home in passages like this one:

How ungenerously in later life we disclaim the virtuous moods of our youth, living in retrospect long, summer days of unreflecting dissipation, Dresden figures of pastoral gaiety! Our wisdom, we prefer to think, is all of our own gathering, while, if the truth be told, it is, most of it, the last coin of a legacy that dwindles with time. (1.3.6)

Remember that the older, narrator Charles is telling the story, which means the attitude with which he reflects on his past experiences will largely define the novel's tone. Because in the 1940s he is "homeless, childless, middle-aged, loveless," it is with a sense of longing that he looks back the "Arcadian days" of his youth. The novel may end on an "unusually cheerful" note (see "What's Up With the Ending?"), but narrator Charles is melancholy for the all of his remembrance.

Writing Style

Lush, Lovely, and Full of Enough Semi-Colons and Well-Placed Metaphors to Last You a Lifetime

Brideshead is written with rich, evocative language perfectly suited to the nostalgic nature of Charles's recollections. If you get down to the level of the nitty-gritty, you'll notice that Waugh is no stranger to the semi-colon either – we even found an article devoted entirely to his use of this particular punctuation mark (see "Links"). But the artistic device which most captures our hearts in *Brideshead Revisited* is the metaphor. (Or simile, you nit-picker you.) There was….this one:

She told me later that she had made a kind of note of me in her mind, as, scanning the shelf for a particular book, one will sometimes have one's attention caught by another, take it down, glance at the title page and, saying "I must read that, too, when I've the time," replace it and

continue the search.(1.7.1)

And of course…this little one right here:

His constant, despairing prayer was to be let alone. By the blue waters and rustling palm of his own mind he was happy and harmless as a Polynesian; only when the big ship dropped anchor beyond the coral reef, and the cutter beached in the lagoon, and, up the golden slope that had never known the print of a boot there trod the grim invasion of trader, administrator, missionary and tourist – only then was it time to disinter the archaic weapons of the tribe and sound the drums in the hills; or, more easily, to turn from the sunlit door and lie alone in the darkness, where the impotent, painted deities paraded the walls in vain, and cough his heart out among the rum bottles. (1.5.205)

And it doesn't get much better than that.

What's Up With the Title?

(Note: This section is about the title of the novel, "Brideshead Revisited." For a discussion of the two internal titles, "Book One, Et in Arcadia Ego" and "Book Two, A Twitch Upon the Thread," see Shmoop's "Symbols, Imagery, Allegory.")

Brideshead refers to the country estate where the Flytes live. Charles's relationship with Sebastian is almost eclipsed by his relationship to the Brideshead estate itself. (Notice that, at the start of his recollection, Charles first recounts his initial visit to Brideshead Castle and only then steps back in time to reveal his first meeting with Sebastian.) His dream of marrying Julia is similarly overwhelmed by the possibility of his inheriting the estate. And though the characters around Charles come and go and his relationships with them shift, evolve, and even disintegrate, it is always Brideshead that remains – the frame story is the clearest proof of this.

Part of the reason for Charles's utter fascination with the estate is his profession: he's an artist. He appreciates beauty, and in particular architecture, which we know becomes his specialty. Check out this passage: "I regarded men as something much less than the buildings they made and inhabited, as mere lodgers and short-term sub-lessees of small importance in the long, fruitful life of their homes." Remember also that Charles paints a medallion on the wall of the garden-room at every one of his visits. The house is literally a record of his growth as an artist. So Brideshead itself hits on one big theme in the book: aesthetics.

After you read Charles's "Character Analysis," you should be comfortable with the idea that, for him, art is a religion. Or at least it's his initial substitute for a belief in God. This means that Brideshead – the epitome of architectural beauty and Charles's gateway into a world of aesthetics and art – is very much tied to the second of the novel's central themes: religion.

Lastly, Charles draws a parallel between Brideshead and his younger, happier days. He doesn't consciously become an adult until the moment he drives away from Brideshead. He narrates: "As I drove away and turned back in the car to take what promised to be my last view of the house, I felt that I was leaving part of myself behind. […] I had left behind me – what?

Youth? Adolescence? Romance? The conjuring stuff of these things." This means we can connect Brideshead to another focus of the novel: youth.

All these connections add up to one big conclusion: Charles isn't just "revisiting" Brideshead. He's revisiting everything that Brideshead stands for – his artistic growth, his journey towards Catholicism, his youth, even his romance with Julia. We're not just talking about a building here.

The other thing to address in the title is the little addendum, "The Sacred and Profane Memories of Captain Charles Ryder." "Profane" isn't talking about swear words here – it actually means "secular." So the book is devoted both to the sacred (or religious) and the profane (or non-religious). As the title suggests, religion is…complicated in Brideshead Revisited. Waugh supposedly intended the novel to be a portrait of divine grace, but many believe it is pitted against Catholicism. Charles, initially an agnostic and eventually a Catholic, struggles deeply with both the magnetic pull of religion and the desires of his secular life – both the sacred and the profane.

What's Up With the Epigraph?
"I am not I; thou art not he or she; they are not they."

First of all, it's not an epigraph – it's the author's note. But we figured this is as good a place as any to talk about it and, besides, it functions a bit like an epigraph; it's just that the quote is from the author himself, not from another source. (Think of it as an egotistical epigraph.)

So what's up with the author's note? This here theory seems to be your best bet: Scholar Jane Mulvagh believes that the author's note is Waugh's little way of saying that Brideshead and the Flyte family are not fictional – they are based on a real family and a real estate – Madresfield. (Read all about it here.) If you buy it, then "I am not I; thou art not he or she; they are not they" is the author's way of saying that Charles isn't just Charles, Sebastian isn't just Sebastian, etc. His novel is a mingling of the fictional and the real.

What's Up With the Ending?
Surprise! Charles is now a Catholic. Did you notice? If not, don't worry, because we only get two small clues that Charles has converted by the time he's in the army in the 1940s. The first hint actually comes in the prologue, when an army man named Hooper tells Charles of their new lodgings at Brideshead: "There's a sort of R.C. church attached. I looked in and there was a kind of service going on – just a padre and one old man. I felt very awkward. More in your line than mine." "R.C." means "Roman Catholic," and Hooper's comment that it's "more in [Charles's] line than [his]" is the clue we're talking about. (We know, it's subtle, but it's there.) The second comes in the epilogue, and is part of this big ending we're trying to talk about here. Charles enters the chapel and "sa[ys] a prayer, an ancient, newly learned form of words." The "newly learned" bit is our second clue and confirms that Charles has in fact recently converted. This is the twitch upon the thread we've been waiting for. We know that Charles was raised in religion ("I was taken to church weekly as a child" he earlier confessed), so his newfound

Catholicism is actually a *return* to God.

Despite appearances, this conversion doesn't come out of the clear blue sky. It has its roots in Lord Marchmain's death scene, when Charles watches the old man and "suddenly [feels] the longing for a sign, if only of courtesy, if only for the sake of the woman [he] love[s], who [kneels] [...] praying [...] for a sign." To Charles, "it seem[s] so small a thing that was asked, the bare acknowledgment of a present, a nod in the crowd." This is where Charles first drops his anti-religion stance and begins to suspect the presence of a God.

It's also the first place where this odd "actors in a universal tragedy" motif comes up. Charles comments that "all over the world people were on their knees before innumerable crosses, and here the drama was being played again by two men – by one man, rather, and he nearer death than life; the universal drama in which there is only one actor."

Fortunately for you, this leads right into the last big important passage in *Brideshead Revisited*, at the heart of the novel's conclusion:

Something quite remote from anything the builders intended has come out of their work, and out of the fierce little human tragedy in which I played; something none of us thought about at the time: a small red flame – a beaten-copper lamp of deplorable design, relit before the beaten-copper doors of a tabernacle; the flame which the old knights saw from their tombs, which they saw put out; that flame burns again for other soldiers, far from home, farther, in heart, than Acre or Jerusalem. It could not have been lit but for the builders and the tragedians, and there I found it this morning, burning anew among the old stones.

The flame to which Charles refers is the candle that is kept lit at the tabernacle on Catholic altars. In the Catholic tradition, the bread and wine consumed during mass represent the body and blood of Christ. This bread is kept in a special place on the altar and always accompanied by a burning flame signifying the presence of Christ. Charles finds solace in this ever-presence and walks away from the chapel newly buoyed by his visit.

Remember when we talked in "The Book" about *Brideshead*'s stance on religion? Some believe that the novel negatively portrays Catholicism, while others are convinced that the novel shows how everyone – even an agnostic like Charles – finds his way to the grace of God. And remember how in Charles's "Character Analysis" we talk about the way that Charles makes art his own secular religion? Right, well those who think that *Brideshead* is pro-Catholicism argue that Charles's attempt to substitute art for God was wrong and in fact impossible. He comes to learn the error of his ways, leaves art behind, and instead becomes a Catholic. That's why in this passage he is so rejuvenated by the presence of Christ at the altar.

Sounds reasonable, right? Sure, but take a look at that long final passage one more time. Notice anything? "..*a beaten-copper lamp of deplorable design.*". Wait a minute...is Charles talking about art here? Why yes, yes he is. In fact, he's talking about the ugly modern art he sees in the chapel at Brideshead. Remember that a big part of Charles's aesthetic education was leaving behind the modern art he first embraced in his young days at Oxford and concluding that it was "bosh" later in his narrative. He might be a Catholic by the end of the novel, but he is *definitely* still an artist.

What does this mean? If Charles tried to replace God with art, doesn't he have to give up art to truly embrace God? One possible answer is this: Charles doesn't reject art in favor of God; *he finds God through art*. Go back to that passage we talk about in Charles's "Character Analysis," when he says of his painting, "I had felt the brush take life in my hand that afternoon; I had had my finger in the great, succulent pie of creation." That's not blasphemy – that's divine inspiration! Charles experiences God through his work. He may have given up his profession, but he hasn't at all given up the strongest connection he has to God: beauty.

Did You Know?

Trivia

- Remember Sebastian's teddy bear Aloysius? Turns out Waugh based this delightful little eccentricity on one of his friend's at Oxford who indeed carried a stuffed bear ("Archie") around with him. (http://www.abbotshill.freeserve.co.uk/Book1Chapter1.html)
- The scene where Charles, Boy, and Sebastian get arrested and spend the evening drunk in jail is based on Waugh's own experience with…getting arrested and spending the evening drunk in jail. (http://www.abbotshill.freeserve.co.uk/AmBook1Chapter5.html)
- Waugh thought that English Lit was the most useless major in college.(http://www.abbotshill.freeserve.co.uk/Monitor.html#Trade)
- Evelyn Waugh's first wife was also named Evelyn. Friends called them "he-Evelyn and she-Evelyn." (http://www.newpartisan.com/home/sponge-cakes-with-gooseberry-fool-evelyn-waugh-was-odd.html)
- Waugh contributed a recipe to *As We Like It: Cookery Recipes by Famous People*. As you should expect, it had everything to do with booze. Here it is:
  Waugh's Mulled Claret
  Take 6 bottles of red wine (it would be improper to use really fine Bordeaux, but the better the wine, the better the concoction). Any sound claret or burgundy will do. One cupful of water; 2 port glasses of brandy; 1 port glass of ginger wine; 1 orange stuffed with cloves; peel of 2 lemons; 3 sticks of cinnamon; 1 grated nutmeg. Heat in covered cauldron. Do not allow to simmer. Serve hot and keep hot on the hob. Should be drunk at same temperature as tea.(http://www.abbotshill.freeserve.co.uk/)
- Supposedly Waugh based Charles and Sebastian's first inauspicious meeting on an experience of his own (that would be someone puking into his first floor room window, if you haven't read the novel recently). (http://www.abbotshill.freeserve.co.uk/)
- Waugh titled one of his novels *A Handful of Dust* with a line taken from *The Waste Land*, the same poem from which Anthony recites in *Brideshead Revisited*.
- Lewis Carroll's *Alice in Wonderland* was one of Waugh's favorite books. (http://www.abbotshill.freeserve.co.uk/)When he got older, Waugh used to pretend he was hard of hearing so he could carry around an obnoxious two-foot-long ear-trumpet and stave off people he didn't like. (http://www.counterpunch.org/claud04262003.html)
- As a young man, Waugh tried to commit suicide by swimming out to sea and drowning

himself. On the way, he was stung by jellyfish and so returned to shore to nurse his injury.
(http://www.newpartisan.com/home/sponge-cakes-with-gooseberry-fool-evelyn-waugh-was
-odd.html)

- Waugh was once fired from a teaching post for trying to get the matron into bed.
(http://www.newpartisan.com/home/sponge-cakes-with-gooseberry-fool-evelyn-waugh-was
-odd.html)

- It wasn't just alcohol – Waugh was a pretty serious drug user, too. It was a running gag
(except for not being funny at all) for him to declare giving up opiates every Lent.
(http://www.newpartisan.com/home/sponge-cakes-with-gooseberry-fool-evelyn-waugh-was
-odd.html)

- Just like the fictional Charles, Waugh was also in the military and hated it. He was so
unpopular that he needed a guard posted at his door while he slept – to protect him from
his own men.

- After *Brideshead Revisited* was published, Evelyn Waugh wrote a short story called
"Charles Ryder's Schooldays" about Charles's time at Oxford. It was never published.

- Check out paragraphs three and four of the second book of *Brideshead*, where Charles
waxes poetic about the nature of memory. Waugh cut these out when he revised his novel
years after its publication. (http://www.abbotshill.freeserve.co.uk/)

Steaminess Rating

PG-13

We're rating this PG-13, but only because all the sex and alcohol-related words in *Brideshead
Revisited* are at a level of vocabulary too advanced for those under the age of thirteen to
understand. How can you pass up a novel with "Dionysian," "prurient," "dipsomaniac,"
"gerontophile," "roué," "licentious," "pederasty," "crapulous," "succubus," "siren," "louche,"
"jeraboam," and a dash of British sexual slang?

Allusions and Cultural References

Literature and Philosophy

William Shakespeare, *Henry IV* ("Henry's speech on St. Crispin's day") (prologue.31)
Edward Marsh (editor), *Georgian Poetry* (1.1.27)
Compton Mackenzie, *Sinister Street* (1.1.27)
Norman Douglas, *South Wind* (1.1.27)
Gilbert and Sullivan (1.1.2)
Alfred Edward Housman, *A Shropshire Lad: Eminent Victorians* (1.1.27)
T.S. Eliot, *The Wasteland* (1.1.62-5)
Alfred Lord Tennyson, *The Princess* (1.1.66)
Pindar, Orphism (1.2.1, 1.2.21)

Marcel Proust (1.2.25)
André Gide (1.2.25)
Jean Cocteau (1.2.25)
Ronald Firbank (1.2.25)
Antic Hay, by Aldous Huxley (1.2.29)
Maurice Maeterlinck, a Belgian symbolist playwright (1.2.45)
Bernard Shaw, *Plays Unpleasant* (1.2.56)
David Garnett, *Lady into Fox* (1.2.58)
George Byron (1.4.221)
Trilby, by George du Maurier (1.5.21)
Georg Wilhelm Friedrich Hegel (1.5.194)
Marcel Proust, *À la recherche du temps perdu* (The character referenced is Baron Palamède de Charlus, a gay man not open about his sexuality.) (1.5.194)
Lewis Carroll, *Alice in Wonderland* (1.5.204)
G.K. Chesteron, *The Wisdom of Father Brown* (1.5.270)
George Grossmith, *The Diary of a Nobody* (1.6.70, 1.6.198)
J.M. Barrie, *Peter Pan* ("Tinkerbell" is the name of the horse Sebastian takes on the hunt) (1.6.67)
Robert Browning, an English poet (1.8.209)
William Shakespeare, *King Lear* (2.1.226)
John Webster, *The Duchess of Malfi* (2.1.226)
Anton Chekhov (2.1.340)
Jane Austen (2.2.62)
Mary Russell Mitford, an English novelist (2.2.62)
Arthur Rimbaud, a French poet (2.2.63)
William Shakespeare, *Macbeth* (2.3.55)

Mythological References
Xanthus, the river near Troy (prologue.31)
King Arthur (prologue.31)
Demosthenes (1.1.25)
Narcissus (1.2.38)
Penelope (Odysseus's wife in Greek Mythology) (1.7.16)
Aladdin (2.5.50, 175)

Art References
William Morris (1.1.27)
The Earl of Arundel, the first great British art collector, during the early 17th century (1.1.27)
Van Gogh, *Sunflowers* (1.1.27)
Roger Fry, an art critic (1.1.27, 1.4.21)
Edward McKnight Kauffer, an American designer while Charles was at Oxford
Roger Fry's *Vision and Design* (1.1.27)
Cezanne (1.1.29)
Sir Edwin Landseer (1.1.29)
Clive Bell's *Art* (1.1.29)
William Hogarth, a 16th Century British painter ("Hogarthian page boy") (1.2.25)
Sergei Diaghilev (1.2.25)

Constantin Brancusi, pioneered modern abstract sculpture (1.2.33)
Jean Ingres, a French painter (1.2.40)
Sir John Everett Millais, "Bubbles" (1.2.47)
Inigo Jones, an English architect (1.4.5, 1.4.9)
Sir John Soane, an English architect (1.4.13)
Thomas Chippendale, a very famous furniture designer (1.4.13)
Giovanni Piranesi, an Italian architect (1.4.15)
John Ruskin, an art critic (1.4.21)
Jacopo Robusti, a.k.a. "Tintoretto," a Venetian painter. (1.4.178)
Augustus John, a painter of portraits. (1.5.36)
Piabia Francis Picabia, an artist of the French avant-garde (1.6.32)
Eugène Delacroix, a French Romanticist painter (1.6.32)
La Gioconda, another title for the *Mona Lisa* (2.1.131)
Paul Gauguin, a post-impressionist painter (2.2.63)
Titian, a painter of the Italian Renaissance (2.5.108)
Raphael, a painter/architect of the Italian Renaissance (2.5.108)

Culture
Isis magazine, the student mag at Oxford (1.1.2, 1.5.9)
Polly Peachum, a leading opera lady (1.1.27)
Honoré Daumier, a French caricaturist (1.1.54)
George du Maurier, "Mrs. Ponsonby de Tomkyns" – a fictional cartoon character (1.2.37)
Punch – a weekly satirical magazine in England (no longer in publication) (1.2.37)
Madame Récamier (1777-1849), an early 19th century French socialite (1.2.45)
Lionel Tennyson, a cricket player and grandson to the great poet (1.4.44)
The Times of London (1.4.44, 1.6.201, 1.7.154, 1.8.196, 2.5.104)
News of the World – A British tabloid (1.4.58)
"Max" refers to William Maxwell Aitken, an influential man in politics and society. (1.5.36)
"F.E." refers to F.E. Smith, the Earl of Birkenhead and a statesman (1.5.36)
"Gertie" Lawrence refers to Gertrude Lawrence, an actor/singer (1.5.36)
Georges Carpentier, a French boxer (1.5.36)
The Star, a former London newspaper (1.5.158)
Vogue (1.6.32)
Continental Daily Mail, a conservative London newspaper (1.6.300)
The Morning Post (1.7.154)
The Blackbirds of 1926, a jazz revue (1.8.10)
Warning Shadows, a German silent movie from 1923 (1.8.25)
Florence Mills, a singer from the <u>jazz age</u> (1.8.28, 37)
The *Tatler* (2.1.97)
Captain Foulenough, a fictional character from *By the Way*, a long-running series in the *Daily Express* of London (2.1.205-211)
Popeye (2.1.211)
Wallis Warfield Simpson (2.2.35)
The *Tatler* (2.2.43)

Military and Political History
Adolf Hitler (prologue.5)

Prince Rupert of the Rhine (prologue.31)
"The Epitaph at Thermopylae" – this epitaph reads: "Stranger, announce to the Spartans that we here lie dead, obedient to their words." (prologue.31)
Bartolomeo Colleoni, general of the Venetian state in the 15th century. (1.4.221)
The Prince of Wales, later King Edward VIII (1.5.36)
Mustapha Kemal Atatürk, founder of the Republic of Turkey (1.6.5)
Miklós Horthy, the Regent of Hungary during World War II (1.8.9)
Abdul Krim, a political revolutionary in Morocco in the 1920s (1.8.83)

Religion
John Henry Cardinal Newman (1.1.2)
St. Nichodemus of Thyatira (1.2.16)
Sodom and Gomorrah – two sinful cities destroyed by God (1.2.45)
Saint Augustine of Hippo, *Confessions* – Sebastian quotes this modified line: "God, make me good – but not yet" (1.4.56)
St. Anthony of Padua (1.4.68)
Saint Francis Xavier, a 16th Century missionary (Cordelia's pig takes this name) (1.4.96)
Jacques Maritain, a Catholic philosopher. (1.5.194)
The Madonna (1.5.201)
St. Joseph (1.5.201)
Father Brown, "The Queer Feet" – The quotation which refers to a "twitch upon the thread" comes from this story. (1.8.194)
Gethsemane (2.5.52)
"Quomodo sedet sola civitas" (1.8.192, 2.1.101, epilogue.55)
"Vanity of vanities, all is vanity," from the Book of Ecclesiastes (epilogue.55)

Historical Figures
Sigmund Freud (1.1.33)Galileo Galilei (1.8.209)

Best of the Web

Movie or TV Productions
2008 Movie, starring Emma Thompson
http://www.imdb.com/title/tt0412536/
They seem to have completely misinterpreted the book as the story of a poor boy ingratiated with a rich family.

1981 Miniseries
http://www.imdb.com/title/tt0083390/
Starring Jeremy Irons as Charles Ryder.

Videos

Sebastian at his plover-egg-eating finest.
http://www.youtube.com/watch?v=LIgwiKxEMI8&feature=related
Clip from the 1981 miniseries.

Trailer for the 2008 film
http://www.apple.com/trailers/miramax/brideshearevisited/
Clearly nothing at all like the novel we all just read.

Images

Evelyn Waugh
http://www.nytimes.com/books/99/10/10/specials/waugh.1.jpg
At age 26 in this painting.

Book Cover
http://g-ec2.images-amazon.com/images/I/51201VYCSHL.jpg
Sebastian would love this font.

Charles, Sebastian, and the real star – Aloysius.
http://www.bbc.co.uk/cambridgeshire/content/images/2007/08/03/brideshead_revisited_itv_203x_152.jpg
From the 1981 miniseries with Jeremy Irons.

Documents

Full Online Text of *Brideshead Revisited*
http://www.kulichki.com/moshkow/WO/brajdshed_engl.txt
Yes, the title is in Russian, but are you really going to complain about free Waugh?

Time Magazine, Waugh's Obituary
http://www.time.com/time/magazine/article/0,9171,899186,00.html
And they call him an "intellectual dandy"!

A Biography
http://www.newpartisan.com/home/sponge-cakes-with-gooseberry-fool-evelyn-waugh-was-odd.html
They only included the weird stuff from Waugh's life. That's still a lot of stuff.

"Fierce Little Tragedy"
http://www.time.com/time/magazine/article/0,9171,797785-1,00.html
Time Magazine's 1946 review of *Brideshead Revisited*.

Websites

A (free!) Online Companion to *Brideshead Revisited*
http://www.abbotshill.freeserve.co.uk/AmContents.html
Absolutely phenomenal. Do not miss this site. It includes a chronological timeline of the events

in the novel, re-ordered from the way they appear in the text, and explanations of all those juicy historical references sprinkled throughout the novel, broken down chapter-by-chapter.

All That Slang
http://www.peetm.com/OxfordTerms.htm
An alphabetized dictionary of Oxford-related slang. Trust us, you'll need it.

"Waugh in his Own Words"
http://www.abbotshill.freeserve.co.uk/HisOwnWords.html
Transcripts from interviews with the author.

Waugh, "The Shakespeare of the semicolon"
http://www.boston.com/news/globe/ideas/brainiac/2007/04/supercomma_sere_1.html
Explores the hallmark of Waugh's writing style